MALCOLM LOWRY:
Vancouver Days

MALCOLM LOWRY:
Vancouver Days

Sheryl Salloum

Harbour Publishing Co. Ltd.
1987

For Kirk

Malcolm Lowry: Vancouver Days
Copyright © Sheryl Salloum 1987

Published by Harbour Publishing Co. Ltd.
Box 219, Madeira Park, BC
Canada V0N 2H0

Cover painting by A.J. Spilsbury
Maps by Gaye Hammond
Printed and bound in Canada by Friesen Printers
Publishing Assistance: Canada Council

Cataloging in Publication Data

Salloum, Sheryl, 1950 –
    Malcolm Lowry

    Includes index.
    Bibliography: p.
    ISBN 0-920080-42-1

    1. Lowry, Malcolm, 1909 – 1957 – Homes and haunts – British
Columbia – Vancouver. I. Title.
PS8523.087Z85 1987   823'.912   C87-091139-2
PR6023.096Z85 1987

Contents

Acknowledgements

Research for this book depended on a wide variety of sources including: Lowry's writings; excerpts from other Lowry biographies, previously published recollections, and academic studies of Lowry's works; correspondence from, and/or interviews with, Lowry's relatives, friends, and acquaintances; and pertinent information related to the history of the Vancouver area.

I wish to thank Literistic Ltd. for giving permission to reprint from the following published material in copyright:
Hear us O Lord from heaven thy dwelling place © 1961 by Margerie Bonner Lowry.
Selected Letters of Malcolm Lowry © 1965 by Margerie Bonner Lowry.
Under the Volcano © 1965 by Margerie Bonner Lowry.
Dark as the Grave Wherein my Friend is Laid © 1968 by Margerie Bonner Lowry.
Review of *Notes From the Century Before: A Journal From British Columbia* © 1969 by Margerie Bonner Lowry.
October Ferry to Gabriola © 1970 by Margerie Bonner Lowry.
Psalms and Songs © 1975 by Margerie Bonner Lowry.

I wish to thank the following for giving permission to quote from published material in copyright:
Mary Aiken and *Canadian Literature* for an extract from Conrad Aiken's "Malcolm Lowry: A Note"; Earle Birney and *Poetry Canada Review* for an extract from "The Unknown Poetry of Malcolm Lowry"; Gordon Bowker, Ariel Books (British Broadcasting Company), Russell Lowry, and Robert Duncan for extracts from Bowker's 1983 interview with Russell Lowry, and Robert Duncan's 1975 interview with Jan Gabrial, as published in *Malcolm Lowry Remembered*; Cambridge University Press for extracts from M.C. Bradbrook's *Malcolm Lowry: His Art and Early Life*; City Lights Books for permission to reprint "Happiness" and "Sestina in a Cantina" from *Selected Poems of Malcolm Lowry* © 1962 by Margerie Lowry; Tony Kilgallin and Press Porcépic for extracts from *Lowry*; *The London Evening News* for an extract from its 14 May 1927 issue; Oxford University Press for extracts from Douglas Day's *Malcolm Lowry: A Biography*; Gerald Noxon for extracts from his recollections of

Lowry as published in *The Malcolm Lowry Review*; Al Purdy and McClelland and Stewart for an extract from *No Other Country*; Al Purdy and *Books in Canada* for an extract from "Lowry: A Memoir"; Vision Press and Russell Lowry for extracts from Anne Smith's *The Art of Malcolm Lowry*; *The Province* newspaper for permission to reprint Lowry's 1939 articles "Hollywood and the War," "The Real Mr. Chips," and "Where Did That One Go To 'Erbert?"; *The Vancouver Sun* newspaper for extracts; and the University of British Columbia Press for an extract from Sherrill Grace's *The Voyage That Never Ends: Malcolm Lowry's Fiction*.

Special thanks to the many contributors who generously granted me interviews and/or permission to reprint correspondence, photographs, and/or recollections: Earle Birney, who not only shared his memories, but also made available his papers and photographs that are housed in the Fisher Rare Book Library, University of Toronto; the late Percy Cummins, Marjorie Kirk, Curt Lang, Arthur McConnell, William McConnell, Alfred McKee, Ben Maartman, George Meckling, Norman Newton, Gloria Onley, George Robertson, Noel Stone, Hilda and Phil Thomas; and those who wish to remain anonymous. I would especially like to thank William McConnell for permission to reprint his short story, "In Search of the Word," and George Robertson for allowing me to view and quote an excerpt from his 1961 CBC television production *Malcolm Lowry: The Forest Path*. To the Dollarton residents who generously granted me interviews, and who helped me piece together the history of the area, my sincere thanks: Mrs. J. Craig, Mrs. J. Massey and the late Mr. C. Massey, Mr. R. Stirrat Sr., as well as those who wish to remain anonymous.

Warm thanks to all those who, in a variety of ways, helped me in the preparation of my manuscript: Dr. Peter Buitenhuis for awakening my interest in Lowry's works, and for encouraging me to investigate Lowry's life in Vancouver; Dr. Sherrill Grace for her continued support; Anne Yandle and the staff of the Special Collections Library, University of British Columbia; Dr. Betty Moss for her correspondence on behalf of Margerie Lowry; Priscilla Woolfan, Margerie Lowry's sister and Conservator, for granting me permission to reprint a number of photographs from the Special Collections Library (U.B.C.), as well as photographs from Margerie's private collection; Pam and Bill Damon for their assistance regarding research in Nanaimo and on Gabriola Island; Mrs. Ruth Darling for a photograph of, as well as information regarding, the Anderson Lodge on Gabriola Island; Robert

McKay, Melody Geddert, and Gary Salloum for their much appreciated comments and enthusiasm; Gaye Hammond, for drawing my maps; and my editor, Audrey McClellan, for her comments and advice.

Other assistance came from the Nanaimo Centennial Museum, June Thompson of the North Shore Museum and Archives, Shell Canada Limited, the Thomas Fisher Rare Book Library of the University of Toronto, the staff of the Historical Photographs Division of the Vancouver Public Library, and the staff of the Corporation of the District of North Vancouver, particularly Mr. Geoffrey Williams and Mr. Des Smith.

Loving thanks to my family for their faith and enthusiasm. Above all I am grateful to my husband, to whom this book is dedicated, for reading and discussing the manuscript with me, and for sharing my appreciation of, and enthusiasm for, Lowry's artistry.

Introduction

Malcolm Lowry was bedeviled by the desire to drink and the desire to write. He began doing both while in his adolescence and continued, in spite of periodic bouts of abstinence, until his death. A prodigious drinker, he consumed bottles of gin, rum, beer, wine, mescal, and other liquors. A prodigious writer, he was intoxicated by the joy, wonder, and power of language. Lowry spent years interweaving images, ideas, and themes into each of his works and planned to further integrate these into a unified body entitled *The Voyage That Never Ends*. Unfortunately, his opus was never finished. Although a number of his works have been printed posthumously, Lowry published only two novels in his lifetime (*Ultramarine*, 1933; *Under the Volcano*, 1947), leaving a considerable volume of "Work in Progress" at the time of his death.

Lowry's artistry was as complex as his personality and both were inextricably interwoven. Since his death in 1957 the mystique of a genius destroyed by alcoholism and deep-rooted psychological problems has developed. Although he did have numerous periods of sobriety, happiness, stability, and industry, any portrayal of Lowry necessitates an attempt to understand his obsession with drinking and writing — his daemons.

Alcoholism is based on psychological, physiological, and socio-cultural conditions. With these factors in mind, Lowry's drinking can be understood as a chronic disorder which may have resulted from: parental deprivation in his early childhood; a physiochemical responsiveness to alcohol; an identification with the image of the alienated, tormented artist; and a family and socio-cultural milieu that caused him to develop feelings of ambivalence, conflict, and guilt. Like many alcoholics, Lowry began drinking at an early age. He was often to become preoccupied by, and unable to control, his drinking and, despite a seemingly outgoing personality, harboured feelings of extreme shyness, insecurity, and sensitivity. His alcoholism sometimes caused angry and violent outbursts and adversely affected many relationships and situations. It worsened a troubled relationship with his father and distanced his family; was the main cause of the failure of his first marriage and often strained his second; caused behavior that he was ashamed of when sober, inducing feelings of inadequacy and depression; and threatened to destroy his creative abilities. Lowry struggled against his alcohol dependency, suffering remorse and despondency when he was not successful, and the traumas of alcohol withdrawal when he was. He described his struggles as "billows of inexhaustible anguish haunted by the insatiable albatross of self."[1] Writing also made immense demands on Lowry's mental and physical being. The need to express his artistic vision was consuming and caused him additional insecurities and anguish. He wrote:

> I have willed one thing and the daemon has decided another.... I can master my booze, my bad temper, my self-deceit, and to some extent my other myriad bad habits, but I have not yet learned how to master that bugger. And if he was a good one it would be different. But he is slow, confused, paranoiac, gruesome of mind, as well as being completely implacable, and he seems to have some vices unknown even to me.[2]

Apart from a six month position as a deckhand on a freighter, writing was Lowry's only employment. For years he made next to nothing from his work and had to live on a remittance from his father. He suffered the repeated rejections of publishers, which intensified his feelings of inferiority and his fear that he would never be a writer of renown. Caught in the orb of his own personality, these feelings not only led him to drink but were in turn augmented by his drinking.

Long hours of writing also brought him physical discomfort. His idiosyncratic method of composing—he stood, leaning on the backs of his hands for long periods—caused him to develop varicose veins as well as heavy callouses on the backs of his hands. A British Columbia doctor likened these callouses to "anthropoid pads."[3]

Lowry persevered and in 1947 received acclaim for the novel that had taken him ten years to write, *Under the Volcano*. His new notoriety meant literary gatherings and book promotions which the diffident Lowry found overwhelming. He drank to cope but became so intoxicated he was either unmanageable or withdrawn. The renown he had yearned for proved traumatic, and in a poem titled "After publication of *Under the Volcano*" he described success as "some horrible disaster."[4]

Initially the novel sold well and was on the *New York Times* "Best-Sellers List" (April and May 1947), but enthusiasm for it declined and so did Lowry's royalties. As much as he disliked success, Lowry paradoxically came to abhor the lack of it. He was not to receive further acclaim as a writer in his lifetime, nor much in the way of income. He continued to write, interrupted by bouts of drinking and emotional exhaustion, until his death on 26 June 1957. Only a handful of friends, along with his wife Margerie and brother Stuart, attended the funeral.

Recognition of Lowry's work began to grow in the 1960s. In Canada he was posthumously awarded the 1961 Governor General's Award for Literature for *Hear us O Lord from heaven thy dwelling place*, a collection of six short stories and a novella, "The Forest Path to the Spring." He has since come to be regarded as one of the greatest writers of the twentieth century. His books, particularly *Under the Volcano*, have been translated into many languages. In 1984 John Huston produced the movie *Under the Volcano*, based on Guy Gallo's screenplay. It starred Albert Finney, Jacqueline Bissett, and Anthony Andrews. The movie premiered at the 1984 Cannes Film Festival.

Lowry's works have influenced musicians, artists, and writers of many nations: British jazz musician Graham Collier, Mexican painter Alberto Gironella, Canadian artist Ron Bolt, Columbian writer Gabriel García Márquez, American writer David Markson, the Canadian writers Robert Kroetsch, Sharon Thesen, and Michael Mercer, to name only a few. Mercer's play *Goodnight Disgrace* is based on the relationship between Lowry and his mentor, the American writer Conrad Aiken. It had its world premiere at the 1984 Shakespeare Plus Festival in Nanaimo, B.C. In 1985 it was again included in the Shakespeare Plus Festival, and then had successful runs in both Vancouver and Toronto.

Lowry has also had an impact on the world's academic community, with numerous theses and dissertations written on his works. The "London Conference on Malcolm Lowry" was held at the University of London, England in 1984; the first "International Malcolm Lowry Symposium" will take place in Canada, at the University of British Columbia, in May 1987.

Lowry drew upon his own personal history as inspiration for his writing. The main characters in his fiction reflect aspects of his personality and poignantly express his thoughts and sentiments. Like his works, Lowry's life was intense, complicated, colourful, and often creatively fabricated. In the way that he re-worked his writings, Lowry "re-worked" aspects of his life, embellishing events to make them more dramatic, and to cultivate the image of a suffering artist. As with his books, it takes more than one "reading" to penetrate the protean aspects of Lowry's character. To date three biographies have undertaken the task: Douglas Day's *Malcolm*

Lowry: A Biography; Muriel Bradbrook's *Malcolm Lowry: His Art and Early Life*; and Gordon Bowker's *Malcolm Lowry Remembered*.[5] These works illustrate the multifarious aspects of Lowry's personality: introverted, theatrical, dispirited, waggish, charming, churlish, powerful, vulnerable, sober, bacchanalian, generous, self-possessed, mystical and ingenious.

Despite the wealth of information that has been provided, Lowry's life in the Vancouver area (1939 – 1954) has not been examined in detail and is the focus of this book. The Vancouver years are significant for they stand out as the most creative and productive of Lowry's career, and as those in which he attained his greatest personal happiness and sense of fulfillment. Descriptions of the area pervade the majority of his writings and inspired or enhanced numerous images and themes. Although he only came to know a small number of people in the area, his friends, like the landscape, were to provide him with inspiration, support, and joy. In turn his Vancouver friends and acquaintances have been left with indelible memories of a unique and endearing individual. Through their recollections, as well as through maps, correspondence, and photographs, Lowry's personality and his life in Vancouver will be highlighted. Before delving into the years 1939 – 1954, however, his life prior to Vancouver must be outlined as it had important and lasting influences on Lowry's personality and artistic vision.

Chapter One

The Formative Years

Clarence Malcolm Lowry, born 28 July 1909, in New Brighton, Cheshire, England, was the youngest son of Evelyn Boden Lowry and Arthur O. Lowry. Methodists, they raised their four sons in an austere environment devoid of many entertainments or displays of affection. Arthur Lowry "never made a friend of" his sons,[1] and in adulthood Malcolm was to complain that his father had made him feel like an "item on the business agenda, even, in some respects, an expendable item" (*Selected Letters*, 260). A successful businessman with interests in cotton and oil, Arthur Lowry travelled extensively and was often accompanied by his wife. Evelyn Lowry had "a complicated but blank relationship" with her sons,[2] and was largely absent in their lives, "except to preside at meals."[3] Left to the care of nannies, Lowry developed feelings of abandonment and neglect that, although often exaggerated, were to afflict him the rest of his life. These feelings contributed to problematic relations with his parents which were never resolved.

His brothers Stuart, Wilfrid, and Russell were respectively fourteen, nine, and four years older than Lowry. Under the influence of their father the three older boys were physically adept and active while the pre-adolescent Lowry was "fat, clumsy, and inept at any sort of physical activity."[4] Although he was to become muscular and physically stronger than Russell, his inability to keep up to or compete with his brothers in his early childhood may have caused some of the feelings of inferiority that were to characterize his personality in later years.

In 1911 the Lowry family moved to Caldy in the Wirral area of Cheshire. A woman who grew up as a neighbour relates that Lowry never quite fit into his family and likens his upbringing to that of "a duckling in a chicken's clutch."[5] She remembers that Arthur Lowry was fond of hunting and often organized weekend "shooting parties." Unlike his brothers, Lowry never wished to participate, causing some contention between him and his father. The same woman recalls that Lowry had a tremendous sense of humour and mischief. Once while she was reading Chaucer with a group of friends, Lowry, who was older than the others, "quite seriously corrected a mispronunciation, then in his dry wit added some hilarious, slightly derogatory comments." On another occasion she remembers sailing with friends down the River Dee, towing Lowry behind in a seatless dingy. He had provided himself with a perch, a chamber pot on which he sat unceremoniously. Those in the sailboat thought it was "a great joke and very daring for those days."

When he was seven Lowry was sent to Caldicott boarding school. During his seven years there he developed corneal ulcers which he claimed left him "half-blind" for three or four years. He also said that his mother refused to allow him home on school vacations because she could not stand the sight of his bandaged eyes. Russell Lowry points out that his brother only suffered from the ulcers for a short time and was then taken to a specialist who quickly relieved the condition. Furthermore, his mother never refused to see him. Lowry did suffer from the painful and disfiguring affliction of chilblains which made his hands look "like bunches of burst sausages"[6] and which contributed to his clumsiness. This ailment does not seem to have been openly discussed by Lowry; however some of his characters convey embarrassment over their small, clumsy hands.

The young Lowry also endured bullying and teasing, particularly as a Cub Scout. The baiting may have been due to his awkwardness or to his quick temper which turned his face red, earning him the nickname "Lobs," short for Lobster. Bradbrook notes that Lowry was harassed by one schoolmaster and often had to bear the sting of his riding switch; he was also ridiculed for his loud passing of wind during sleep.[7] While the taunting was probably common fare, he found it demoralizing, and, despite his later exaggerations, his feelings of suffering, neglect and deprivation were no doubt real. In adulthood Lowry expressed the loneliness and anguish of his schoolboy days in a poem:

> An autopsy on this childhood then reveals
> That he was flayed at seven, crucified at eleven,
> And he was blind besides and jeered at
> For his blindness.[8]

At this time Lowry was developing idiosyncrasies which were later to influence him as a writer. He began to exhibit an interest in foreign or strange words, signs, occurrences, and hymns. He also exhibited a phenomenal memory for these and, according to Russell, would "bank" them, "especially obscure or unusual words.... His joy was...boundless if he could find a use for some rare item in his collection." Another characteristic which developed at an early age was an "absorption which took no account of time, while he was playing with words."[9]

When he was fourteen Lowry attended a public school in Cambridge, the Leys, which had "a definite religious air about it. Students in Lowry's day assembled for prayers twice daily during the week, and attended both morning and evening church services on Sundays."[10] Despite the strict regimen, Lowry's personality began to unfold. He acted in two of the school's dramatic productions, *Tilly of Bloomsbury* and *Oliver Cromwell*; interest in, and a flare for, the theatrical were to become lifelong characteristics. He also found an expressive outlet in writing and became noted for his acrid coverage of the school's hockey games. Under the psuedonyms CML and CAMEL he published short prose as well as light verse in the school magazine, *The Fortnightly.*[11]

Lowry had grown into a stocky adolescent and became active in weight lifting, swimming, tennis, rugger, as well as golf, which he came to play expertly. He won medals in two tournaments hosted by the Royal Liverpool Golf Club: in 1923 for boys under fifteen, with a score of 95; in 1925 for boys fifteen to eighteen, with a score of 88. However, he was not the "champion" he later claimed to be. Years after a schoolboys' championship tournament, Russell learned that his then fifteen or sixteen year old brother had in fact been too drunk to compete.[12]

While at the Leys Lowry gained some notoriety as a musician. He played a small ukulele, which he called a taropatch, and formed a friendship with another student, Ronald Hill, who played the piano. They preferred hot jazz tunes including one called "Hindu Babe," to which Lowry added accompaniment by passing wind in the rhythmic breaks. The two youths did some composing and their fathers financed the printing of two of their tunes: "Three Little Dog-Gone Mice: Just the Latest Charleston Fox-trot Ever" and "I've said Goodbye to Shanghai."[13]

Although Lowry did not excel academically, his father expected him to attend Cambridge University when he graduated from the Leys in 1927. The unconventional youth had other ideas and convinced his father that he should first go to sea. Using his influence, Arthur Lowry arranged for his son to sign onto the Blue Funnel freighter *Pyrrhus* as a deckhand. When his parents drove him to the dockside, on 15 May 1927, they were greeted by reporters who quoted Lowry as saying, "No silk-cushion youth for me, I want to see the world, and rub shoulders with its oddities, and get some experience of life before I go back to Cambridge University."[14] It was also reported that he was taking his ukulele and planned to compose new Charlestons. Unknown to anyone at the time, Lowry had arranged for the publicity himself in the hopes that it would bolster his reputation as a musician and writer. The publicity did not have the desired effects; in fact it probably caused some of the difficulties he encountered with the ship's crew. Obviously from a different class and background, Lowry met with distrust, contempt, and harassment for the duration of the near six month voyage.[15]

His romantic notions of a sailor's life quickly dissipated as he discovered that he was not only a lonely misfit but that work on a freighter was tedious; his tasks included chipping paint and rust from winches, and hauling ashes from the stokehold. His experiences at sea did provide a rich background for fiction, and from the time of his return home in October 1927, through his subsequent years at Cambridge (1929 – 1932), Lowry worked at writing his first novel, *Ultramarine.*

Dissatisfied with his beginning drafts, Lowry looked for exemplary works based on the traditions of the sea. He was impressed with the novels of two contemporaries: *Blue Voyage* by the American writer Conrad Aiken, which Lowry considered "the work of a poet"; and *The Ship Sails On* by the Norwegian writer Nordahl Grieg, which Lowry considered the work of a poet and dramatist. His desire to become a "poetic dramatist" was greatly influenced by the work of these men. Drawn to both he stated, "the aim of my psyche seems to have been to make a synthesis of these two factors [poetry and drama]" (*Selected Letters*, 265).

Not much is known of Lowry's relationship with Grieg other than that he voyaged to Norway to meet him in the summer of 1930. Lowry told differing and obviously exaggerated versions of this trip: in one he claimed to have worked as a fireman on a Norwegian freighter to earn his passage; in another he said he had jumped ship in Oslo and then trekked to the north of Norway with only the aid of a compass and map. He further embellished his quest by claiming that Grieg lived under an assumed name and that his address was only discovered through a series of coincidences.[16] Letters written to Grieg indicate that the two did meet, and the trip provided Lowry with background material for a second manuscript, "In Ballast to the White Sea."

In 1929 Lowry wrote Aiken a letter of admiration in which he asked to be taken on as a student. Aiken agreed and Lowry sailed to Cambridge, Massachusetts, where Aiken had a temporary summer teaching appointment. On the evening of his arrival, Lowry and Aiken got roaring drunk and wrestled for the possession of an unusual trophy, a porcelain toilet seat. In the struggle Lowry threw Aiken against the stone fireplace, causing a skull fracture and a permanent scar in the shape of a cross.[17] According to Aiken the two were "astonishingly en rapport."[18] In between bouts of alcoholic revelry, Lowry spent the summer working on *Ultramarine* under Aiken's tutelage.

Lowry returned to England and entered St. Catharine's College, Cambridge, in the autumn of 1927. He graduated with a Tripos in English in 1932. He was not as interested in his studies as he was in visiting Aiken (who had returned to his dwelling in Rye, Sussex); working on *Ultramarine*; playing his taropatch; listening to, and developing a lasting fascination with, American jazz, particularly the music of Bix Beiderbecke, Eddie Lang, Frankie Trumbauer, and Joe Venuti; drinking in the local pubs, and keeping company with his new found intellectual friends who gathered regularly at the "addled salon" of Charlotte Haldane, the wife of a Cambridge professor.[19] Russell recalls that during this time his brother was becoming more and more rebellious, drunken, and aggressive, and that Lowry's increasingly violent and eccentric behavior began to strain his family relationships. In one angry disagreement over Lowry's drunken behaviour, he and Russell came to blows, leaving a permanent schism between them.[20] Increasingly intolerant of his son's behaviour and attitudes, Arthur Lowry paid Aiken, who was later to state that he and Malcolm were "uncannily alike in almost everything," to act *in loco parentis.*[21]

One incident from his Cambridge days stands out as having deeply affected Lowry: a fellow student, Paul Launcelot Charles Fitte, committed suicide by coal gas poisoning. The 16 November 1929 issue of the *Cambridge Daily News* reported that "Clement Milton Lowry" was the last person to see Fitte alive. From Lowry's testimony, and other evidence presented at the inquest, it appears that Fitte was distraught over gambling debts for which he was possibly being blackmailed. He was also unhappy at Cambridge and depressed over a car accident. Lowry testified that Fitte had mentioned taking his own life, but Lowry had not taken him seriously. Lowry was to convey Fitte's death differently to Margerie and friends: he described Fitte as a homosexual who had pursued him and then threatened suicide if Lowry continued to spurn him. How much truth there is to this version is not known, but feelings of remorse and guilt over Fitte's death were to plague Lowry for years to come. The character Wensleydale who appears in drafts of three of Lowry's works, as well as the character Peter Cordwainer in *October Ferry to Gabriola*, are modelled on Paul Fitte and his death; the protagonists of these works are consumed with guilt over a friend's death.[22]

The years 1933 to 1939 were tempestuous for Lowry. When *Ultramarine* was completed he submitted his only draft to the publishing company Chatto and Windus. A suitcase containing the draft was stolen from the back seat of the car of one of the editors, Ian Parsons. The manuscript was never recovered and Lowry was faced with having to rewrite it from memory. In an attempt to recapture aspects of the novel he desperately revisited the various places at which he had worked on it. Luckily his friend Martin Case had saved a discarded draft from which Lowry was able to rewrite the manuscript. Lowry told Parsons he only wanted the novel to be accepted if it was deserving, and not because of the loss of the manuscript.[23] In the end the novel was rejected by Chatto and Windus, but was published by Jonathan Cape in 1933 (a revised edition was published by Cape in 1963).

In March 1933 Conrad and Clarissa Aiken invited Lowry to accompany them on a trip to Spain. While there he met and fell in love with an American woman, Jan Gabrial, whom he married on 6 January 1934. From the beginning their relationship was turbulent and they quarrelled often, including the morning of their wedding. Lowry's drinking and Jan's sense of independence added further stresses to their relationship. According to Jan they fluctuated between "good periods, difficult periods, good periods, difficult periods."[24]

They made plans to settle in France, where they both intended to work at writing, but first Jan travelled alone to the United States in April 1934. The trip was apparently made to notify her mother of her marriage, but by July she still had not returned, indicating an already unworkable and unhappy relationship. Lowry decided to join her and they settled in New York where, between continued bouts of quarrelling and drinking, Lowry worked on "In Ballast to the White Sea." Their relationship worsened and eventually he and Jan separated.

Distraught, Lowry began to drink so heavily that his health seemed endangered. In 1936 a friend named Eric Estorick took Lowry to a psychiatrist and he was voluntarily admitted to Bellevue Hospital.[25] He recovered quickly and his ten day experience in Bellevue became the basis for the posthumously published novella *Lunar Caustic*.

Unfortunately the state of his marriage did not improve; it continued to deteriorate. Jan and Lowry travelled to Los Angeles for a month, and in December 1936 they moved to Cuernavaca, Mexico. Inspired by the Mexican landscape Lowry began work on *Under the Volcano*. The friction between the Lowrys fluctuated, as did Lowry's drinking, until Jan felt they had reached the point where they "were talking past each other."[26] She left Lowry in December 1937 and returned to Los Angeles.

Her departure was catastrophic for Lowry and he began drinking uncontrollably. He travelled to Oaxaca toward the end of December and there spent the nine day Christmas celebration in jail for drunkenness and for what may have been politically unacceptable statements; he wrote Aiken that he had been imprisoned as a "spy." In the same letter he described the degree of his physical and emotional despair: "Have now reached condition of amnesia, breakdown, heartbreak, consumption, cholera, alcoholic poisoning, and God will not like to know what else, if he has to, which is damned doubtful" (*Selected Letters*, 15). Reports of Lowry's condition, his growing accumulation of debts, and the cessation of diplomatic relations between England and Mexico in 1938, caused Arthur Lowry to pay his son's outstanding bills and to arrange his departure from the country.

Despite the chaos and emotional upheaval of the years 1934 – 1938, especially during the time in Mexico, Lowry had absorbed an array of sensations and perceptions and was developing them into the symbols, metaphors, and narrative levels that characterize his work. He had started the novella based on his stay in Bellevue, continued working on the sea novel that had begun to take shape in 1930, and while in Mexico he completed a first draft of *Under the Volcano* and began work on a second draft.

By most standards, particularly those of his father, the nearly thirty year old Lowry had accomplished little, other than a scandalous reputation. When he arrived in Los Angeles in June 1938, Lowry found that his father had placed him under the supervision of a Los Angeles attorney, Benjamin Parks, who declared Lowry an "incompetent." Lowry spent the next year working on his writings, including a number of poems inspired by Mexico, and completed the second draft of *Under the Volcano*. He also met Margerie Bonner, with whom he immediately fell in love.

In June 1939 Benjamin Parks told Lowry that he had to leave the country in order to renew his visa. Travel to Mexico was out of the question so a trip to Vancouver, Canada, was arranged. According to Day, Lowry could have renewed his visa in Los Angeles but Arthur Lowry wanted his son relocated.[27] Parks drove Lowry to Vancouver and there turned him over to the supervision of a Canadian attorney, A.B. Carey. Unbeknownst to Lowry, Vancouver was to be more than a stopover. It was to have a significant influence on his life.

Chapter Two
Vancouver Days

Although Lowry came to feel a deep attachment to the Vancouver area, initially he abhorred it. He found the city, which was only fifty-three years old in 1939, to be provincial, and wrote that it had "a sort of Pango Pango quality mingled with sausage and mash and generally a rather Puritan atmosphere. Everyone fast asleep and when you prick them a Union Jack flows out of the hole."[1] The city was also industrial. Lowry found the many sawmills offensive and described them as "relentlessly smoking and champing away like demons."[2] He was appalled by the social degradation in the city's Skid Road area, and disliked the beer parlours that sold "beer so weak no self-respecting drunkard would show his nose in them."[3] He was even more distressed at being separated from Margerie Bonner and the only copy of his second draft of *Under the Volcano* — both were in Los Angeles.

Lowry endured for one month in what he called "the most hopeless of all cities of the lost" (*Selected Letters*, 20), then, in a state of inebriation, he set out for Los Angeles via a bus to Seattle,

Bus for Seattle leaving the Motor Transport Building (Dunsmuir and Seymour) in Vancouver, similiar to the bus Lowry took in 1939. (Circa 1936. Vancouver Public Library #10672.)

9

Washington. As a result of his drunkenness (and no doubt his shortage of funds) he was refused entry to the United States at the Blaine Border Crossing. His plight was immediately worsened as it was then necessary to wait one year before another application for re-entry could be made. Hearing this, Margerie decided to join Lowry in Vancouver.

When she arrived in August 1939, she found him living in the attic room of a house belonging to Maurice Carey on West 19th Avenue (Map 1). In a letter to Conrad Aiken, Lowry described their living quarters:

> Now the setup is this: $2 a week for myself and Margerie in return for which we get one meal a day if we're lucky. There is a family of six, including a loud speaker, a howling wind which rages through the house all day, twins, and a nurse. I forgot the dog, the canary and a Hindoo timber merchant,... who sleeps in the woodpile in the basement, hoping, with his fine Oriental calm, that one day he'll be paid for the wood (*Selected Letters*, 20).

Lowry was unhappy with his surroundings but was unable to leave: the remittance from Arthur Lowry was being sent to the Los Angeles lawyer Benjamin Parks, who in turn forwarded it to A.B. Carey, who then passed it on to Lowry's landlord Maurice Carey (the two Careys were not related).

Over the next nine months Lowry desperately sought to escape both the Carey household and Vancouver. He complained to his father that he was being exploited and neglected by his new guardian, as well as by his landlord, and begged to be allowed to move to Toronto or Montreal in order to be closer to Conrad Aiken who could again act *in loco parentis*. He also pleaded with his father to let him manage his own affairs, arguing that he had not been drinking and, despite the "noise and confusion" of his surroundings, was working "like the very devil himself...[and] writing simultaneously on several books" (U.B.C. 1:79). Arthur Lowry was out of patience with his son and unsympathetic to his plight. He wrote that he felt Malcolm could live reasonably well in Vancouver and he did not wish to pay for "all sorts of fresh arrangements" (U.B.C. 1:38).

In an attempt to supplement his finances, Lowry wrote three articles for the *Vancouver Daily Province*, which were published in its 12, 13, and 29 December 1939 issues, earning him $30.00 (Appendix 2). These articles highlight aspects of Lowry's personality, particularly his wit, as well as his feelings toward the disquieting events that were leading to the Second World War. They also demonstrate Lowry's use of dramatic and cinematic techniques, and the unconventional perspectives he presented to the Vancouver readership of 1939.[4]

Lowry sent the articles to his father to prove that he had not been "entirely idle," and complained that he could not work regularly because he had "no status." He further argued, "Besides, I have more serious work to do which will net me more money in the long run." Lowry also sent his father a letter he had received from John Buchan, Lord Tweedsmuir, the Governor General of Canada, and pleaded, "If a man who was second only to the King could treat me lately as a personal friend, encouraged me and admired my writing,...would you countenance reports which still doubtless brand me as an incompetent, fit only for a drunkard's home, not to be trusted?" (U.B.C. 1:79).

By May 1940 Arthur Lowry had decided to let his nearly thirty-one year old son "have the chance partly to manage" his own affairs, and wrote that the $100.00 a month remittance would be sent directly to him if he would "shew some contrition for...past treatment of your father and mother," and if the "itemised accounts" Lowry was to send home indicated he could "resume the responsibilities of a normal life again" (U.B.C. 1:38). The English treasury was beginning to place restrictions on funds leaving England, however, and it appears that from the end of May 1940 until April 1942 there were few remittances from Arthur Lowry. It is not clear what Malcolm and Margerie lived on in that time, but Arthur Lowry's letters of 7 May and 31 May 1940 indicate that he may have arranged, through connections in the United States, to send Malcolm a few pounds sterling every month (U.B.C. 1:38).

With the cessation of the remittance, Lowry was finally freed from the Carey household, and in May 1940 he and Margerie found more comfortable and pleasant lodgings in the home of Mr. and Mrs. J.D. Smith, on West 11th Avenue (Map 1). Through the upheaval of the past nine months, Lowry had been working steadily on a revised draft of the *Volcano* manuscript which had arrived safely from Los Angeles. This draft was completed at the Smiths', and Lowry was optimistic that it would be published. However, *Under the Volcano* was not to be accepted for publication until 1946 and "was refused by no fewer than thirteen publishers in 1940 – 41."[5]

In August 1940, despite their restricted finances, Lowry and Margerie rented a squatter's shack for a month long vacation on the foreshore of Burrard Inlet near the village of Dollarton. Captivated by the ever-changing seascape, abundant wildlife, "primeval forest," and seclusion, Lowry and Margerie felt they had found a life style that was "dying out of the world" (*Selected Letters*, 314). Dollarton was to be their home for the better part of the next fourteen years.

The landscape had a vitalizing impact on Lowry, and its "conjunction of favoring yet opposing circumstances"[6] came to have personal and artistic significance for him; as a result, descriptions of the landscape were incorporated into the majority of his writings. Moreover, the events that shaped Dollarton, from its isolated and industrialized beginnings of 1916 to its development as a suburban, residential community in the 1950s, had a peripheral but important effect on Lowry's life.

Dollarton originated as an offshoot of Vancouver's flourishing logging and sawmilling industry which in 1914 had the greatest density of lumber mills in western Canada.[7] The Vancouver Lumber Company owned and operated a mill in Burrard Inlet, northeast of Roche Point. In 1916 the Canadian Robert Dollar Company built a sawmill and dock adjacent to the Vancouver Cedar Mill (Map 2). According to the *Memoirs of Robert Dollar* the company

> bought 100 acres of land... and built a modern, up-to-date saw mill, especially constructed to supply our China trade.... Then we had to lay out a village, and build houses for our employees.... Each house has a garden and the rent of $15.00 a month includes water, electricity and wood. A postoffice, with a daily mail service has been established, which is called Dollarton. Dollarton also has a church, the minister being on our pay roll, and a school.[8]

In 1929 the Vancouver Cedar Mill and the Dollar Mill ceased operations due to the effects of the Depression. The Cedar Mill never reopened and was eventually dismantled. The Dollar Mill reopened in 1932 and operated until 1943, when the mill and its timber rights were sold to other interests.[9] The new owners closed the mill and it too was dismantled.

When the Dollar Mill first opened, there were no bridges connecting Vancouver with the North Shore, making Dollarton accessible only by boat. Some people rowed across the inlet and some used the service provided by the Harbour Navigation Company.[10] Dollarton could not be reached by road until 1918, when the Dollar Road was built to Keith Road (Map 2), giving Dollarton residents road access to Deep Cove and North

A ship loading lumber at the Dollar Mill. The mill housing can be seen in the background, as well as the tank that supplied the mill and the village with water. The large building on the right served as a bunkhouse. The Dollarton Highway is beyond the trees. (Circa 1939. Vancouver Public Library #6504.)

Panorama of North Vancouver and the Second Narrows Railway Bridge over Burrard Inlet. Dollarton is off to the right. (Circa 1940. Vancouver Public Library #10140.)

Vancouver. In 1925 the Second Narrows Railway Bridge was opened, substantially increasing highway and rail traffic to North Vancouver. The route to Dollarton remained circuitous until the opening of the Dollarton Highway in 1930. With the improved access came new industries and a gradual increase in the population of the Dollarton/Deep Cove area.

Over the years shipping in Burrard Inlet, east of the Second Narrows, became increasingly active. Two shipping related industries were founded on the north side of the inlet, west of Dollarton: McKenzie Derrick (1930), later to be known as McKenzie Barge and Marineways,[11] and Matsumoto Shipyards (1949). In 1932 the Shellburn refinery was built in Burnaby on the south side of Burrard Inlet (Map 2) and "was to become the centre for both the refining and marketing sections of Shell in B.C."[12] During the Second World War the refinery produced 5000 barrels of gasoline per day. The refinery expanded in 1946 with the addition of a thermal cracking unit, a polymerization unit, a re-run unit that was used to improve the production of motor gasoline, a new steam boiler house, and eighteen new storage tanks; in 1948 a new crude fractionating tower increased production to 9000 barrels of crude per day.

The Shellburn refinery was highly visible from the squatters' shacks on the opposite shore of the inlet. Concerned over its visual, auditory, and environmental impact, Lowry often harangued against the refinery. He was particularly disturbed when a "gruesome carpet of dirty oil" would spread across the inlet, despoiling the beach and killing marine life.[13] As Bradbrook points out, Lowry's environmental awareness and "his crusade against pollution" were far ahead of the times.[14] Descriptions of the refinery as a vision of Hell that constantly threatens the paradisial qualities of the Dollarton beach, Lowry's "Eridanus," are to be found in many of his writings. He also used hellish images to symbolize the demonic elements that constantly threaten the human soul.

Small dwellings began to appear near Roche Point in the early 1930s (Map 3). Some were shelter for those suffering the effects of the Depression, a few were temporary homes for men working at the local mills and McKenzie Barge, and some were cheap and accessible housing for fishermen. "Old Sam" Miller and Whitey (Miles Went) were two fishermen who first erected dwellings near Roche Point. Built on pilings, they were situated on property that belonged to the Vancouver Harbour Board, and came to be known as "squatters' shacks." By the early 1950s the number of shacks had

Shellburn Refinery. (Circa 1960. Courtesy of Shell Canada Limited.)

A fiendish lurid light coruscated from the whole refinery, each of whose cylindrical aluminum tanks reflecting the flambeaux in descending degrees of infernal brilliance, in turn sent those reflections wavering deep within the dark stream.... Those luminescent digladiations gave at first the impression of taking place in sinister silence but in fact there was a hellish if magnificent din.... While they watched and listened, a coarse cerise light switched on, illuminating in large capitals erected against the grass slope below—someone having omitted to supply the initial S—the word HELL. (October Ferry to Gabriola, 159.)

The Seven Sisters, Stanley Park. (Circa 1928. Vancouver Public Library #4558.)

In the park of the seaport the giant trees swayed, and taller than any were the tragic Seven Sisters, a constellation of seven noble red cedars that had grown there for hundreds of years, but were now dying, blasted, with bare peeled tops and stricken boughs. (They were dying rather than live longer near civilization....) ("The Bravest Boat," Hear us O Lord from heaven thy dwelling place, *13.)*

increased to approximately ninety. Few people were to live on the beach as long as the Lowrys, and in the 1940s and 1950s most of the shacks were used for summer vacation cabins.

Mr. and Mrs. James (Jimmy) Craige also settled on the beach. Jimmy, who had apprenticed as a boat builder in the Isle of Man, constructed a boat shed as "large as a small church" next to his shack, and there helped his sons build a fishing boat.[15] Jimmy Craige's sons and daughters also built on the beach. Marjorie Kirk (daughter of Jimmy Craige and wife of Lowry's friend Downie Kirk) recalls that one or two of the shacks were

> quite well built, almost like a real home...[but most of the shacks were] usually a little bit jerry-built....[They] were not really what one would call comfortable....Most of the shacks tended to have castaways and leftovers from something that nobody needed at home....To us it [shack] was always something said in a loving way, "Let's go to the shack," because it was the highlight of the year....It was very pleasant there in the summertime with the beach right at your door and the woods right at your back. It was just something gorgeous.[16]

The entrance to Stanley Park. (Circa 1939. Vancouver Public Library #6244.)

> *A five-car lane: but who wanted a five-car lane to a park that would end by being logged and a five-car lane itself. More deathscape, more potlust — bah! (October Ferry to Gabriola, 188.)*

The Caileag Gheal *(White Lady) was built by Jimmy Craige and his sons in Craige's Dollarton boat shed. (Courtesy of Jean Craig.)*

> *Then all at once a fishing boat with tall gear comes running round the point like a white giraffe, very swift and stately, leaving directly behind it a long silver scalloped rim of wake. (*Under the Volcano, *37.)*

The Lowrys rented their first shack from a group of Scotsmen who used it during fishing trips. The shack had two rooms, outdoor plumbing, and was heated by a wood cook stove. They paid $15.00 to rent the shack from mid-August to mid-September but, when the month was up, decided to stay on; they then paid an off-season monthly rate of $7.50.[17]

The next four years were close to idyllic. Lowry's divorce was finalized and he and Margerie were married on 2 December 1940. They lived a reclusive life and when Lowry was not writing they spent their time swimming, going out in their rowboat, doing daily chores, bird watching, and enjoying the ocean vista outside their door.

The couple developed a warm and symbiotic relationship with Sam, Whitey, and Jimmy. They gave each other companionship, and, through the practical knowledge and experience of these men, the Lowrys learned to adapt to their environment. Journals and other writings indicate that the Lowrys helped Sam and Whitey to caulk and paint their fishing boats, and that they kept watch over the fishermen's shacks in their absences. Lowry incorporated Sam, Whitey, and Jimmy into "The Forest Path to the Spring," using them as models for the characters Mauger, Kristbjorg, and Quaggan.

It was the fatherly figure of Jimmy Craige to whom the Lowrys became the most attached. According to Marjorie Kirk, Jimmy shared a fondness for cats with Margerie and a fondness for seagulls with Lowry. Jimmy also liked spiders and was the model for Guillard, a man who kept spiders as "pets," in Margerie's mystery novel *The Shapes That Creep*. During the Lowrys' absences from the beach, Jimmy watched over their "beloved shack" and often prepared it for their return. In one letter Lowry recounts how Jimmy had dried their wet mattress with hot bricks, making it "a warm as well as a happy homecoming" (*Selected Letters*, 306).

In March 1941 the Lowrys purchased a shack for $100.00 and by May had cleaned, repaired, and moved into it. Ecstatic at owning their own home "they painted the door red, and the window frames yellow."[18] With the help of Sam and Jimmy they also constructed a pier that, despite its ramshackle appearance, withstood the tides, storms, and logs that were hurled against it. The "brave pier" came to have a special significance for Lowry. He likened the fragile structure's paradoxical strength to the psychological stamina of humankind, which must also weather a myriad of stresses. Lowry wrote that the pier "was not as might first appear a barren symbol, for it was capable, if not of infinite, of continual extension,... and while it had the strongest of foundations, it possessed also the lightest of structures, and yet had borne the most violent tempests."[19]

Like the pier, Malcolm and Margerie's marriage was to weather many storms. In one journal Margerie wrote:

> Yesterday was bad...what lunacy—we yowled & spat like 2 starving dogs over a bone over my idea for a poem on the summer solstice. I was frantic with pain—but now it seems to me it would make a very amusing short story (U.B.C.21:8).

The Lowrys' second shack was purchased in 1941 for $100.00 and was destroyed by fire in 1944. (Courtesy of Margerie Lowry.)

As Lowry put it, Margerie was "the right gal" (*Selected Letters*, 23). Her devotion, support, and practicality were to prove indispensable. Not only did she do all his typing, she also made notes on their travels and daily life, and became a valuable consultant and editor. Numerous pages in Lowry's manuscripts contain notes to "see Margie" or to "use Margie's note," and she sometimes wrote a "Margie version."[20] The influence of her descriptive abilities and her sense of narrative pacing are evident in many of Lowry's works.[21] She became a successful writer herself. In 1944 – 1945 she wrote several radio scripts for the C.B.C. and collaborated with Lowry on a radio dramatization of *Moby Dick*, a film script of *Tender is the Night* (neither have been produced to date[22]), and a short story which Lowry was to re-work into the

Lowry standing on the Dollarton beach in 1944. (Special Collections Library, University of British Columbia, BC 1614/6.)

novel *October Ferry to Gabriola*. She published three novels with Scribner's: *The Last Twist of the Knife* (1946), *The Shapes That Creep* (1946), and *Horse in the Sky* (1947). A fourth novel, "The Castle of Malatesta," was never published, but the manuscript is held at U.B.C. Since Lowry's death, Margerie has fostered her husband's reputation by editing, alone and with others, a number of his unfinished works, his *Selected Letters*, as well as reminiscences and criticism.

From 1940 to 1944 the Lowrys revelled in their new environment. Malcolm drank in moderation and swam daily in warm weather. He and Margerie enjoyed walks in the forest; they viewed a continual panorama of sea vessels, sunrises, and sunsets, developed interests in local plant and animal life, became ardent bird watchers, and enjoyed rowboat trips and picnics. One of Margerie's journals recounts a fifty mile "jaunt" up a fork in Burrard Inlet known as Indian Arm, in which "Malcolm rowed the whole way." She described it as "one more adventure shared, one more experience of beauty we had known together" (U.B.C. 21:8).

In those years Lowry was physically and emotionally fit, and worked diligently on *Under the Volcano*. In Dollarton, Lowry made significant additions and changes, shaping the novel into a work "so designed, counterdesigned and interwelded that it could be read an indefinite number of times and still not have yielded all its meaning or its drama or its poetry" (*Selected Letters*, 88). The novel is layered with literary allusions and devices, including allegory, metaphor, and mythical imagery. Interwoven are themes that highlight the psychic struggles of humankind: the struggle to overcome feelings of guilt and alienation; to communicate in a fragmented society; to demonstrate love and human charity; to cope with historical and political injustices and suffering; and to overcome physical and emotional impairments (such as dip-somania) in order to attain spiritual salvation.

Under the Volcano is set in Mexico, a lost and decaying paradise, but contains descriptions of a northern home that offers the characters hope for physical, spiritual, and artistic fulfillment. The Dollarton landscape undoubtedly influenced Lowry's portrayal of this Edenic setting. He also used it to convey an important aspect of the novel: hope that the characters and, on another level, humankind could cross their spiritual abyss to attain psychic equilibrium.

Another of the novel's motifs was inspired by a man whom Lowry met in 1942. Charles Stansfeld-Jones lived close to Dollarton, in Deep Cove. Also known as Frater Achad, Stansfeld-Jones had published two Cabbalistic texts, *The Reception of the Bride* and *Anatomy of the Body*. He instructed Lowry in the mystical teachings of the Cabbala. Lowry used this knowledge to deepen the spiritual depths of the novel.[23]

The harmony of the Lowrys' life was ruptured on the morning of 7 June 1944 when a fire broke out in their shack. Lowry ran to a home in Dollarton (the first house from the beach) to ask that the occupants phone the fire department. The owner remembers, "Lowry was shouting, 'Help, help, help me!' He was only dressed in his undershorts and he was gasping and holding his stomach in such a way that I thought he'd been stabbed." The home did not have a phone, so Lowry ran to the general store owned by Percy Cummins, who recalls: "I grabbed some pails and a pump and ran down to the shack. The neighbours were packin' water while I was pumpin', tryin' to put the fire out. After the fire I took them up to my house and gave them tea and my wife, Ethel, fixed them a meal."[24] Due to its inaccessibility, it was impossible for efficient fire fighting equipment to reach the shack, and it was lost.

The Lowrys rescued some of their belongings and most of Malcolm's writings. Unfortunately, all but a dozen or so pages of "In Ballast to the White Sea," the novel Lowry had been working on since 1930, were lost; the novel was never rewritten. Burns on Lowry's back were the only physical injuries resulting from the fire, but both he and Margerie were emotionally devastated by their loss.

They stayed a few nights in the homes of friends, and then Jimmy Craige offered them lodging in the shack belonging to Jimmy's daughter and son-in-law, Marjorie and Downie Kirk. After a few weeks had passed, the Lowrys were still too disturbed to stay in Dollarton and went to stay with a Cambridge friend of Malcolm's, Gerald Noxon, who was living in Ontario. It was there that Lowry completed *Under the Volcano*.

Gerald Noxon had known Lowry since 1929 when both were university students. As was often the case with Lowry and his friends, the two did not see much of one another, but Noxon, whom Lowry referred to as his "first editor," was to cross paths with him in Canada and proved an invaluable friend. The following recollections are taken from a tape-recorded rehearsal copy of a radio broadcast Noxon made in the United States in 1961:

> I was publishing a small...undergraduate literary and art magazine called *Experiment*, and, of course, we were soliciting contributions from all students in the university....At that time Malcolm was engaged in writing a novel called *Ultramarine*....I think everybody was agreed on the editorial board of the magazine...that here was a writer of talent.
>
> Exactly how this talent was going to work itself out it was quite impossible to say at that time, because Malcolm did have certain very grave literary problems to solve, as well as many other problems of a personal nature....But one of his great problems from a literary point of view at that time was — as with most writers who are starting their first serious work — it was to evolve a style, a way of writing which would be reasonably consistent with what he had to say, the subject matter that he wanted to deal with, and the breadth and scope of his understanding....
>
> During the Cambridge days most of my contacts with Malcolm Lowry were of a purely literary nature....I didn't see very much of

him and when I did. . . it was usually to discuss a specific piece of work or to try to get him to put down on paper things which he had discussed;. . . the kind of thing that most publishers have to do: to try to extract copy from an author for whose work they have considerable regard.

However, it must have been in the fall of 1930. . . that quite accidentally I was in the town of Rye, in Sussex, and I ran into Malcolm on the street. . . . I found out that he was staying with Conrad Aiken. . . . I was staying for several days in the neighbourhood and much of this time Malcolm and I spent together going around from one pub to another, of which there is an incredible number in even so small a place as Rye, and going swimming out off Camber sands. During that period. . . we didn't talk much about books, we talked more about places and ideas in general — I felt that during those few days I got to know him very much better than I had ever known him up at Cambridge and I became more than ever conscious of the problems which he had to solve as a person, and, also, I gathered some of the reasons for these problems, which were of long standing and arising out of his childhood. . . .

Anyway, it was an extremely revealing and extraordinarily fascinating time as far as I was concerned. And I began to understand the directions in which Malcolm's talent might lead him if he were able to achieve a sufficient degree of stability to become the writer that he so obviously was capable of becoming. . . .

After that occasion I saw very little of him. . . . It was not until I came to Canada, after the first year of the war, and after working briefly for the National Film Board. I began to write many documentary radio broadcasts for the C.B.C., and work on these broadcasts took me to Vancouver on at least three separate occasions. . . [and] on three occasions I saw Malcolm.

He was not an easy man to find there. I knew that he lived in a little shack on the shores of Burrard Inlet, but I had to find out from asking locals where this could possibly be, and it was only after some difficulty that I learned that it must be at Dollarton that he was living. I had no idea what to expect of Dollarton: it was a name on the map and that was about all, and it was very hard to get there. I believe it was by bus that I finally got to the store at Dollarton, which was, oh, perhaps a quarter or half a mile from the place where Malcolm lived. And I had to ask at the store, which was also the post office, and there, of course, Malcolm and his second wife, Margerie, were well known: they got all their supplies from the store and visited it almost every day. There was a path down through the forest — very large trees and very wonderful forest growth — that led down to the shore from the little store; for the first time I really wondered whether I would find Malcolm Lowry at the end of this trip or not.

Finally, however, I did find him, living in a small shack built up on stilts at the front end, and sort of nestling into the steep bank of the forest at the back, a little two-room affair — at least one room and one very small appendage or second room. . . . There was a deck around one side of it, and . . . a dock, or rather a catwalk that Malcolm had constructed, built out over the rocks, so that a row-boat which he had could be kept out there free of the rocks at low tide and also where it was possible to swim from when the tide was up — the big tide. . . . I just wondered whether it would come up high enough to lift. . . the whole place, bodily away and take it out into the inlet.

I had not intended to stay the night with them. . . but I became so fascinated with Malcolm's account of what he was doing, which was in effect writing *Under the Volcano*, that I stayed over, and we spent most of the night in discussing the book and its problems. He read me very large portions of it and was most anxious to know what I thought about it since he had been more or less out of touch with people who could sit and listen to him and in whose judgement he had a certain amount of faith. He had been working more or less in the dark.[25]

Now at this time Malcolm's personal life seemed to have straightened out tremendously and he was working very hard on the book. I remember on the. . . first visit he read me the very wonderful opening chapter of the book and asked me for criticisms about it and this was rather difficult for me to do because I had really no grasp of the work as a whole or of the extraordinarily significant part which this opening chapter was to have in the work as a whole.

However, we did discuss for many hours the very opening sentence of the book, and we re-wrote it together perhaps twenty times until it assumed the shape which it has in the novel today. The difficulty was — and this was the old difficulty as far as Malcolm was concerned — that he wanted a first sentence of such extraordinary and monumental nature, he wanted to include so much information, such a broad vista, such a broad picture, and all in one sentence, that I told him that this was simply unreadable the way he had put it down and — whereas it was quite clear to me. . . that Malcolm was never going to be a writer of simple, uncomplicated, sort of Hemingway-style writing — this was going a little bit too far. In effect, we broke down what he had originally written in one sentence into three. . . .

In the same kind of way. . . we went over many other parts of the book which had, even at that time, . . . achieved the main features which it was later to show, although a tremendous amount of rewriting had still to be done.

Much of this was, in my opinion, not absolutely necessary, and I think one has to realize that while there was an admirable side to Malcolm's perfectionism about what he was writing, that sometimes he re-worked material to a point where it began to lose its vitality. . . . There was no telling as to what the result would be: sometimes it was good and sometimes it wasn't.

After that initial visit to Dollarton I kept in fairly frequent touch by letter with Malcolm, [and] the progress of the book. I returned to Dollarton on two other occasions... during which time we were taken up not only with the *Volcano* but also with other stories and projects which Malcolm had in hand, including a book the manuscript of which was eventually destroyed in a fire—"In Ballast to the White Sea"....

I was living... at Oakville, on Lake Ontario, and one morning I got a telegram from Malcolm saying that the shack... had burnt down, that they had lost all their possessions, that they were broke, that they had nowhere to go, and that he himself was suffering from burns, and could I possibly raise enough money to get them to come east where perhaps something could be worked out. I might say that Malcolm, all through the years that he was in Vancouver, was receiving a very small allowance from his family. This was small for many reasons... [and the] overriding one [was] simply that people were not allowed to send money out of England in any but the very smallest quantities, so he never had any reserve whatsoever. Fortunately, at the time I had some spare money around and I sent him enough to get himself and Margerie east to our place on the train and they duly arrived in what was a pretty appalling condition.

The manuscript of the book, "In Ballast to the White Sea," had been lost, burned in the fire. The manuscript of the *Volcano* had fortunately been saved in toto. Some other manuscripts had been either destroyed or lost—it was impossible to tell—but as far as I was concerned the great thing was that the *Volcano* manuscript had been preserved.

Malcolm was suffering from very severe burns on his back where a blazing log had fallen on him as he had left the cabin trying to rescue the manuscripts. He had received treatment for this, but it was a number of weeks before he really became calm.... He was extremely agitated... because one has to understand that his world was one of extraordinary superstition. Everything that happened was a portent, and a fearful one usually. There were at the back of his mind visions of the most appalling nature and the symbolism of this fire.... Incidentally, those shacks along the inlet—they were always burning down—it was almost to be expected; they were constructed in such a way that if a flue from a stove got a little bit too hot or something, a fire was virtually inevitable. So, there was nothing extraordinary about that from most people's point of view, but for Malcolm this was really not only a disaster but a portentous happening which he would never be able to completely recover from, he felt.

Malcolm had started to work again on the *Volcano*.... (He was now doing entirely revision work. The book was virtually completed.... But he still had things that he wanted to do in connection with it and so there was no gainsaying him.) However,... he had just begun to recover from his physical condition and to get into a better sort of mental shape, able to work, when one day...I heard that a Norwegian...writer by the name of Nordahl Grieg had been killed while acting as an observer in a British bomber over Berlin. He had made the trip simply in order to be able to write about the experience, and the plane had been shot down....For some reason, I had not known up to this time of the influence that this Nordahl Grieg had had on Malcolm in Malcolm's early years. Either he had not told me about this or if he had told me I had not connected that Nordahl Grieg with the one whose death had just been announced and it was really by the purest chance that I happened to mention this. This fell like a thunderbolt and this was another of this terrible concatenation of events which to Malcolm was starting to spell out doom. So it really set him back to where he was before—really nothing more unfortunate could have happened just at that time—and it began to look as if the *Volcano* again might never see completion.

About that time I bought a house across Lake Ontario at Niagara-on-the-Lake....The Lowrys, who had been staying in our home in Oakville—which was a large sort of place—then moved over to Niagara-on-the-Lake with us and they took a small, very small house there and it was there that the *Volcano* finally was completed.[26] And it was on Christmas of 1944 that the thing was finally typed and sent off to the publisher and Malcolm presented me with the manuscript, the manuscript of that particular version, which is pretty near to the way it was finally published.

At any rate, he considered it at that time completed. It was sent off to publishers and Malcolm and Margerie then returned to British Columbia.[27]

Malcolm and Margerie in front of their house at Niagara-on-the-Lake, Ontario, 1944. (Courtesy of Margerie Lowry.)

In February 1945, the Lowrys re-rented their first shack and, with the help of Jimmy, began to rebuild their burned home. They purchased the lumber and windows from the defunct Dollar Mill, and constructed a two room dwelling. According to Vancouver friends, the bedroom had a curtain which served as a door, and the room was just wide enough for their bed — a double mattress on the floor; the kitchen/living room had the appearance of two rooms due to a book shelf that also served as a room divider. Marjorie Kirk remembers that the shack was "crude but interesting. It had everything they needed and was artistically furnished, even though they didn't have much."

Shortly after the shack was finished, the Lowrys received their first notice of eviction from the Vancouver Harbour Board. It was soon followed by a reprieve. In 1946 their eviction again seemed imminent and the Lowrys travelled to Vancouver and Gabriola Islands in the hopes of finding another inexpensive seaside home. Notes made on this trip were developed into a jointly written short story, "October Ferry to Gabriola," which Lowry later began to expand into a novel. They returned home to find that the squatters had received another reprieve. However, life in Dollarton was

The Lowrys' third shack was built in 1945 on the same location as the second. The room at the back is the bedroom. (Courtesy of Margerie Lowry.)

changing due to development of the community. "Progress" and eviction notices were to threaten the Burrard Inlet paradise until their final leave-taking in 1954.

Alterations to the landscape began in 1944 (four years after the Lowrys' arrival) when the Dollar Mill property was sold and subdivided for the proposed Roslyn Park Subdivision. In the initial phase of the development the 21 homes on the mill site were renovated and painted, and two new roads, Roslyn Drive and Beach Drive (now Beachview Drive), were constructed. John R. Sigmore Limited of Vancouver listed 161 lots in its sales brochure and by September 1944, 33 of the lots had sold. One lot was reserved for a proposed country club and two others for the club parking lot. Lot prices ranged from $500.00 to $1500.00. Certain restrictions were to be applied. To quote the brochure:

> Title is restricted to members of the white race. . . . No house may be built which is valued at less than three thousand dollars. Houses and trees and shrubs must be so placed so that they will not interfere with the view of other residents.[28]

Considering the alterations to the natural surroundings, the costs of the property and housing, and the developer's restrictions, especially the race restrictions, it is not surprising that Lowry referred to the subdivision as "Dark Rosslyn." The subdivision never reached the stage of development that was advertised, although some lots were sold and some new houses built; the exclusive Seymour Golf and Country Club opened in 1953. Lowry's short story "Gin and Goldenrod" is set in Dollarton in the years 1944 to 1947. It describes the development of the village as destructive and another threat to the Edenic setting. Lowry wrote that there was a

> hideous slash of felled trees, bare, broken, ugly land crossed by dusty roads and dotted with new ugly houses where only a few years ago rested the beautiful forest they had loved. . . . Progress was the enemy. . . . Ruination and vulgarization had become a habit.[29]

Over the years Dollarton locals became more concerned with the fate of the property in the area of the squatters' shacks. Their view that the shacks were unsightly and the squatters undesirable was reinforced by newspaper accounts of other Vancouver squatter communities. Vancouver civic officials disapproved of squatters not paying taxes, and they described the shacks as: "Unbelievably filthy, disease breeding, vermin producing hovels. . . . A nest of perverts."[30] In Dollarton, the squatters of "Lazy Bay" (a name coined by Dollarton residents) came to be viewed with suspicion. One Dollarton old-timer recalls:

> The only squatter I knew about was Lowry. Percy used to get quite upset with him because he couldn't pay his bills. Lowry didn't have a very good reputation, neither did the others. To us they were just squatters. All our men. . . worked and earned their money. These squatters stayed down there and we didn't really know what they did. It was a queer situation.

The Lowrys inadvertently added to the suspicions. Due to their reclusiveness they knew only a few of their fellow squatters, and, according to Percy Cummins, they "had little to do with anyone in Dollarton." News travelled swiftly in the small town, and while the Lowrys kept to themselves, their circumstances and behavior were well known. Overall Lowry was disliked because he was viewed as a "remittance man," a drunk, and an eccentric. One Dollarton resident relates examples of Lowry's behavior which were considered aberrant:

> They were in Percy's store and Margerie was filling his arms with groceries, bread, canned goods, and other necessities. Without warning he opened his arms, letting all the groceries fall, making a real mess on the floor. He just stood there while she cleaned it up.
> Another time I observed them as they rowed up to the Dollar Mill wharf. There was a water tap at the watchman's shack and the Lowrys were coming to get water. Margerie was rowing and when they reached the wharf she couldn't get him to grab onto the dock. There was a sudden downpour and she managed to tie the boat up and ran for cover. She kept yelling at him to "Come ashore," but he just sat in the bow grinning this damn foolish grin. Finally she ran down, helped him out of the boat and to cover.

However, when people came to know the Lowrys, their views often changed. A woman who lived on the beach remembers that she initially thought Margerie was pretentious because of the amount of jewelry she wore, and found both of the Lowrys unusual for their theatrical behaviour:

> I remember being out on a float helping my husband to sort shrimp. Malcolm and Margerie had been away and as soon as they returned they came running down to the Craiges'. Margerie stoc on the steps

as if she was on a stage and cried out "We're here! We're here!" Malcolm was just as theatrical. One night after he'd been drinking he went out on his pier and like an actor on a stage was calling out, "I curse you! I curse you! Go to hell and be damned!" At first I thought he was saying this to the people next door but I later learned it was directed to the refinery.

I once sat with Margerie on the bus to Dollarton and was surprised to find that she was very nice and very down to earth. She seemed interested in the fact that we were building a house. I told her about a log on our property that had a stump on top of it and a tree growing out of the stump. Margerie said, "Just think, when that log was a tree Shakespeare was living and writing!" It was interesting because I had totally different associations with the tree's history—Indians hunting in the dense forest. And from one or two conversations I had with Malcolm, I discovered he was also very nice and that we shared similar interests.

The local children viewed Lowry as a source of entertainment. If they saw the Lowrys get off the bus at Cummins' store, and if it was obvious Malcolm had been drinking, they would hide in the bushes along the trail to watch them make their way home, laughing at Lowry's slipping and falling as he negotiated the steep trail, and Margerie's struggles to keep him upright. Sometimes they were also frightened by Lowry and one individual recalls:

> Someone once told him to put socks on over his boots when it snowed so he wouldn't slip on the steep trail. But he wore them over his boots all the time. I remember seeing him in the middle of the summer wearing a fur coat and boots. He was drunk and he scared me.

There was some concern that the young people in Dollarton might come in contact with the squatters. Although their fears were never substantiated, the parents worried that their children would have access to alcohol and "whatever else went on down there." However, it seems that the squatters had more to fear than the Dollarton residents. From various recollections it is known that adolescents often caused damage to the homes of the squatters, overturning outhouses and breaking into the shacks. In one of her journals, Margerie describes how two boys

> wreaked a path of destruction down the beach, breaking into half a dozen houses & polishing off with poor Bells [Map 3] where they have really made a sickening & terrifying mess. . . . Windows smashed, every flower box smashed. . . rain barrel smashed. . . inside the whole floor is

strewn with...matches, sugar, glasses, dishes, spilled ink, branflakes, coal oil poured around, burnt papers...curtains ripped down & the rods broken (U.B.C. 21:8).

The Lowrys themselves were subjected to the mischievous overturning of their outhouse, and to at least one break in. In 1954, after they had left the beach, a group of boys broke down the door of one of their storage shacks, possibly the one they called the "mink's house." The Lowrys had left a large collection of correspondence and manuscripts in the shack, which the boys rifled through. They took some of the papers home and at least one of the boys showed the booty to his parents before it was discarded.[31] It will never be known how many papers were taken in this way, and their contents are lost forever!

Despite the many hardships they had to endure, the Lowrys continued to delight in their seaside home. They were keen observers of the marine life that abounded in the area; mentioned in Lowry's writings are barnacles, crabs, mussels, "little shellfish called Chinese Hats,"[32] seabirds, whales, and seals. In the summer of 1946 the Lowrys found and adopted a young, motherless seal. References to it are found in a letter to Albert Erskine,[33] and in "Present Estate of Pompeii" in which Lowry states:

A baby seal had come swimming up on the beach...[and] fearing it might be threatened or starve without its mother...they'd kept it for several days in their bathtub. This particular day they'd taken the seal for a swim and suddenly, in a flash, it slipped away and was gone. They'd swum after it hopelessly.[34]

According to Stefani Hewlett, marine biologist at the Vancouver Aquarium, the pup was most likely a harbor seal, a small, spotted seal common to the waters of Burrard Inlet. Unlike the young of other members of the seal family, such as the sea lion, harbor seals will tolerate being handled, and seldom bite. Although it is now illegal for a private citizen to care for wildlife, Hewlett says that the Lowrys took appropriate action for the time, and probably saved the animal's life.

Caring for a seal is an arduous undertaking that requires patience and common sense. Like any baby, a young seal needs regular feeding and attention, cannot be house trained, and bawls when hungry or lonely. In order to keep its skin moistened, a seal needs continual access to water. When the water is warm from sitting in a receptacle (such as the Lowrys' bathtub), a seal's muscles will relax, causing it to defecate, and making it necessary to change the water frequently.

Despite the labour involved, the Lowrys seemed to delight in nursing the baby seal. In a book review, Margerie wrote:

> We...fed it milk and then fish and took it out daily for swims. My husband was a remarkable swimmer and he and the seal would frolic about gaily; one day the seal decided he was old enough to be free and he swam away so swiftly that even Malcolm could not catch him, to Malcolm's great chagrin.[35]

The care the Lowrys provided enabled the seal to grow strong and healthy enough to gain its independence. The animal's departure was natural and it could not have understood Lowry's disappointment.

Lowry would have been more crestfallen if he had known that the nurturing he and Margerie had provided for the seal was misconstrued by some Dollarton residents. A local boy, who was ten or eleven at the time, was walking along the beach in front of the Lowrys' shack when they called to him for help to move the seal from the bathtub to the beach—the boy obliged. News of this incident, and the fact that Lowry was inebriated, reinforced the image of Lowry as a drunken eccentric. Rather than an act of conservation, the care the Lowrys had provided for the seal was viewed as further proof of their strangeness.

One Dollarton resident who had regular contact with the Lowrys and an impact on their lives, as well as on the rest of the community, was the storekeeper Percy Cummins. He moved to Dollarton for a job in 1916, and, like many others, felt a great appreciation for the area's natural beauty. Cummins lived and worked in Dollarton until 1966. Initially he laboured in the Dollar Mill, and later was a storekeeper, postmaster, justice of the peace, notary public, and a member of the North Vancouver District Council. Cummins remembers: "In 1929 when all the sawmills shut down I built a store and service station...[on the Dollarton Highway] and I got the post office" (Map 3). The store became a stop for the privately run Deep Cove Stage Lines (the first bus service in the area), as well as for later bus service. Simply called the "General Store," Cummins' became a focal point in the community: people went there to collect their mail, catch the bus, buy groceries, and converse with one another. Lowry and other squatters sometimes hauled water from Percy's tap.

The Cummins' home was situated above the forest that separated the beach from the Dollarton Highway. Fearing housing or industrial development below his property, he began to campaign to have the area designated a park, and soon had the support of the local Ratepayers' Association. In 1949 the Town Planning Commission visited the location of the proposed park area, and with "the guidance of Mr. Percy Cummins...tramped the whole area."[36] Cummins and another Dollarton storekeeper, Robert Stirrat, helped to work out the most suitable area, and the park site was approved. Cates Park, as it is now called, was named after a prominent North Vancouver family that donated property to the site. Over the years the squatters were given notices of eviction from the park site, but it was not until the mid to late 1950s that the District began to bulldoze and burn the shacks; the last shacks were destroyed in 1958.

In the 1940s Lowry ironically lamented that the ramshackle beach houses were to be replaced by "autocamps of the better class" (*Selected Letters*, 50). One such facility, the Heywood Park Auto-Camp (1926 – 1942), was situated on Marine Drive in North Vancouver (Map 1) and Lowry would have passed the site while travelling from Vancouver to Dollarton. For Lowry, auto-camps were personally threatening and offensive. He incorporated this image into his writing and, as he did with the sawmills of "Enochvilleport" (Vancouver) and the Shell refinery, used the image to symbolize a threat to Paradise.

In 1945 Arthur Lowry died from "carcinoma of the rectum."[37] Although his father had been a teetotaller, Malcolm related his death as the result of the alcoholic's disease, cirrhosis of the liver. With the settlement of his father's estate, Lowry received a few thousand dollars, but the rest of his inheritance was held in trust and remitted by his eldest brother Stuart. As their shack was not yet winterized and they could now afford to travel, Lowry decided he and Margerie should spend the winter in Mexico. The manuscript for *Under the Volcano* had been sent to his New York agent, Harold Matson, and, as indicated by Day in *Malcolm Lowry: A Biography*, Lowry wanted to check the Spanish expressions used in the novel, was hoping to find inspiration for a sequel, and wanted to give Margerie a holiday and show her the sights described in the book. They left Vancouver in November 1945, visited with Margerie's family in Los Angeles, and by mid-December were in Mexico.

On 31 December 1945 Lowry received a letter from the British publisher Jonathan Cape, which stated that, while *Under the*

Volcano had "integrity and importance," alterations should be made in order to ensure a "favourable reception" (*Selected Letters*, 425). Despondent, Lowry made a half-hearted attempt to cut his wrists. Within a few days he had pulled himself together and wrote a lengthy letter of rebuttal to the comments of William Plomer, one of Cape's readers.[38] As a result, the novel was accepted without major alterations and was published in 1947.

The trip to Mexico was fraught with other troubling experiences. Visiting his old haunts renewed painful memories which "were all of suffering, hideous anxiety, or the escape from, or more powerfully into, these through tequilla or mescal — of the certainty that his life was falling to pieces."[39] Lowry was shocked and depressed to discover that his old friend Juan Fernando Marquez (the model for Juan Cerillo and Dr. Vigil in *Under the Volcano*) had died, and that his death had occurred in circumstances similar to those surrounding the death of Geoffrey Firmin, the main

Heywood Auto-Camp, North Vancouver, B.C. (Circa 1928. Vancouver Public Library #6288.)

"Auto camps of the better class," their besetting nightmare, they might find when they returned, the forest felled, their own house knocked down and ugliness and an urban subsection beginning to move in. (Dark as the Grave Wherein my Friend is Laid, 34.)

35

character in the novel. In March 1946 Lowry and Margerie encountered problems with the Mexican police over a bill that Lowry apparently still owed from 1938. They were subjected to interrogations and intimidation until May, when they were deported. While these experiences were emotionally devastating, they provided Lowry with background material for two works, *Dark as the Grave Wherein my Friend is Laid*, and "La Mordida" (the bite or bribe) which has never been published.[40]

In 1947 Reynal and Hitchcock (New York) and Jonathan Cape (London) published *Under the Volcano*. After struggling for ten years to write the novel and get it into print, its publication brought Lowry new dilemmas. In one letter, he wrote that "the favorable reviews of the *Volcano* frightened the hell" out of him (*Selected Letters*, 140). However, he was just as fearful of criticism. Upset by one unfavorable review, he sent the critic (Jacques Barzun) a lengthy retort to his "horribly unfair criticism" (*Selected Letters*, 143).

In November 1946 the Lowrys travelled to New York, via New Orleans and Haiti, to take part in book promotions for the American edition. Lowry, characteristically, became absorbed with his new surroundings, finding the rituals of voodoo particularly fascinating, and with a new friend, a writer, Philippe Thoby-Marcelin. According to Day, Lowry also drank "without cessation" in Haiti (possibly in trepidation of the book's reception, positive or negative), and was hospitalized for a week in January 1947. In New York the promotional activities and literary gatherings were more than Lowry could handle. He drank continuously and either evaded gatherings or suffered through them in absolute silence.[41]

The Lowrys returned to Dollarton in March 1947, but life on the beach was no longer as secluded. Lowry was sought out by the local newspapers: the *Vancouver Sun* published an article on the Lowrys in its 17 April 1947 issue, noting them as a "talented writing couple"; on 19 April the *Vancouver Daily Province* reviewed *Under the Volcano* as a "depressing but powerful novel" and one that had "deep significance"; in its 1 August issue the *Vancouver Sun* ran another article entitled "Wealthy Squatters Find Rent-Free Beach Haven." Lowry was described as "a successful novelist who could write a cheque for thousands," and his neighbours on "Royal Row" were described as "a sales manager, a prosperous fisherman, a bank clerk, a dentist, [and] a number of craftsmen."[42] The article did not focus on Lowry or his writing but on the fact that he, like the increasing number of squatters at Roche Point, did not pay taxes.

Although *Under the Volcano* was on the best sellers lists and was an alternate selection for the "Book of the Month Club," and though countries such as Italy, France, and Germany began to buy translation rights, its popularity dwindled as did Lowry's royalties. His main source of income again became the monthly remittance. In November 1947, while still riding the wave of success, the Lowrys went for a fourteen month holiday in Europe, which provided Lowry with inspiration for several short stories.[43] He also drank heavily and, as a result, was hospitalized three times: in a hospital in Vernon, France; in the American Hospital in Paris; and in a sanatorium in Rome.[44] After returning to Dollarton in January 1949, Lowry wrote his friend Clarisse Francillon (also one of the French translators of *Under the Volcano*), and this letter illustrates the immense stabilizing effect the Dollarton environment had on Lowry:

I have made a very strange general recovery.... Delayed in London for 14 hours by storm I drank heavily indeed: innumerable pints of beer, brandy, and rum.... Crossing the Atlantic...I drank innumerable whiskies at the bar and innumerable brandies with...sonoryl [a tranquilizer].... During the colossal flight right across Canada from Montreal to Vancouver liquor was disastrously forbidden on the plane but fortunately we had bought a bottle of excellent whiskey in Montreal of which, with Margerie, I drank about half right under the nose of the snooty stewardess. At Vancouver we went to a pub, drank beer, pouring the rest of the whiskey into it, ate enormously, bought two more bottles of whiskey and went home.... The next morning, although it was freezing, I rose as if automatically, made the fire and the coffee, and breakfasted upon ham and eggs, sonoryl, and the remainder of the whiskey and set off to the store to get food.... My intention was to get a bus at the store, go to town and purchase some more whiskey, which was perhaps a psychological turning point, for instead I returned as soon as possible without any liquor and did not drink for the rest of that day. The next day...I also rose at dawn and did the chores: Margerie purchased some gin, of which we drank a little, but the next day and the next I drank nothing at all.... I also found I had lost my taste for tobacco and practically stopped smoking cigarettes altogether — at most 4 a day instead of 60 or so. We sometimes have a bottle or two of beer, or a few cocktails of gin and fruit juice before dinner, but the craving, the absolute *necessity* for alcohol, has stopped in a way I cannot account for.... What is remarkable in this (and I am experienced) is the complete lack of suffering during this period. For the last year I had averaged at least 2½ litres to 3 litres of red wine a day, to say nothing of other drinks at bars and during my last 2 months in Paris this had increased to about 2 litres of rum per day. Even if it ended up by addling me completely I could not move or think without vast quantities of alcohol, without which, even for a few hours, it was an unimaginable torture. During this last period here in Canada I have waited in vain for the shakes, in vain for D.T.'s, or even worse horrors (*Selected Letters*, 167 – 169).

Lowry settled back into the routine of writing and living on the beach. He did not leave the Vancouver area again until his "eviction" in 1954.

Chapter Three
His Fires Still Burn Fiercely:
Vancouver Remembrances

T he homeliness of life on Burrard Inlet was a tonic to the anxieties that tormented Lowry. He could again cope without vast quantities of alcohol and faced life with high-heartedness; he embarked on a period of creative energy. With Margerie he wrote a screenplay of F. Scott Fitzgerald's novel *Tender Is the Night*. (Although it was considered "brilliant" and a "masterpiece" by numerous playwrights, it was shelved due to its approximate six hour length and because it was not in keeping with the production style of Hollywood.) Lowry worked on a number of manuscripts: a novel length version of the short story he had written with Margerie ("October Ferry to Gabriola"); a collection of novellas under the title *Hear us O Lord from heaven thy dwelling place* – the atmosphere of Dollarton and the Vancouver area, particularly Stanley Park, permeates these works; and his poetry collection, *The Lighthouse Invites the Storm*. Many of his poems depict life in Dollarton and indicate the pleasure, strength, and stimulation he drew from the surroundings. The poem "Happiness" (Appendix 2) poignantly reflects Lowry's appreciation of Dollarton.

In 1951 he wrote his agent Harold Matson that he was planning an interrelated body of novels entitled *The Voyage That Never Ends* (a project he had conceived in 1940 – 41); it would include *Ultramarine, Under the Volcano, Dark as the Grave Wherein my Friend is Laid*, "La Mordida," and *October Ferry to Gabriola*.[1] The opus was still a "Work in Progress" at the time of Lowry's death in 1957.

The years 1949 to 1954 were filled with long spells of writing and continued delight in the natural surroundings, but were encumbered with physical discomforts and financial difficulties. Both Lowry and Margerie suffered physical ailments: in 1949 Lowry had an operation to remove the painful varicose veins in his legs; also in 1949, while Margerie was visiting her family in Los Angeles, he fell from their pier and received "a compression fracture of the fourth dorsal vertebra."[2] Consequently, he had to wear a back brace for the next six months. In June 1953 Lowry tripped on a root while walking up the steep trail from the beach, and fractured both the tibia and fibula of his right leg. This accident caused Margerie

Lost Lagoon, Stanley Park. (Circa 1927. Vancouver Public Library #4611.)

> *It was a day of spindrift and blowing sea-foam, with black clouds presaging rain driven over the mountains from the sea by a wild March wind.*
>
> *But a clean silver sea light came from along the horizon where the sky itself was like glowing silver. ("The Bravest Boat,"* Hear us O Lord from heaven thy dwelling place, *13.)*

injury as well. Rushing to Percy Cummins' to phone the ambulance, Margerie was attacked by his large, ferocious guard dog. Cummins recalls:

> I had a dog that I left in my garage to keep burglars out. The Lowrys often got water at the tap at my pumps. The dog always got after them when they came anywhere near the pumps. Margerie came up to the house to use the phone and I was workin' in my garden, my dog with me. She put up her hands and yelled, "Oh that horrible creature!" That dog remembered her voice and bit her backside.

These two unfortunate events resulted in hospitalization for both Lowry and Margerie. The incident with the dog also strained the Lowrys' relationship with Cummins. He laments, "Margerie never spoke to me after that. They even went away without

Stanley Park, Vancouver. (Circa 1940. Vancouver Public Library #4617.)

> *The pear-shaped lagoon now narrowed to a kind of rustic canal or neck that connected with the shipless bay beyond, bridged by little arched rustic bridges, exquisitely beautiful. ("Ghostkeeper,"* Psalms and Songs, *211.)*

speakin';... after knowing them for several years and carryin' them on my books for a long time."

In his correspondence Lowry indicates that Margerie suffered from worrisome health problems: he mentions that she may have cancer, that she is being x-rayed for a brain tumour, and that her ailments may be due to the aftereffects of a hysterectomy. In other letters he mentions that she is ill and in pain, that her teeth are being affected by a growth, and that she has worms. Although Lowry may have exaggerated the condition of Margerie's health in order to elicit sympathy and/or monies, his concerns were no doubt genuine. Margerie's brother-in-law, Bert Woolfan, was a medical doctor, and on at least one occasion she travelled to Los Angeles to seek his medical opinion and, perhaps, treatment.

The cold weather became more difficult to endure and from 1952 to 1954 the Lowrys spent their winters in Vancouver apartments. The sales of *Under the Volcano* had petered out and the "wealthy

The three Vancouver apartment blocks the Lowrys lived in during the winters of the early 1950s.

a. Kenmore Apartments, 1075 Gilford Street, Apt. 33, the Lowrys' 1952 winter residence. (Circa 1943. Vancouver Public Library #5162.)

b. Bayview Apartment Hotel, 1359 Davie Street, the Lowrys' 1953 winter residence. (Circa 1925. Vancouver Public Library #8955.)

c. Caroline Court Apartments, 1058 Nelson Street, Apt. 73, the Lowrys' 1954 winter residence. (Circa 1940. Vancouver Public Library #5176.)

squatter" found that the winter rents and medical expenses, along with the devaluation of the English pound, were seriously straining his finances. In 1951 he wrote his brother Stuart a "begging letter," asking that his remittance be increased. (It appears that it was not.) Other correspondence indicates that the Lowrys were buying their groceries on credit at Cummins' store, and that they sought emergency loans from numerous friends, as well as advances from publishers. In December 1950 Evelyn Lowry died intestate and Lowry's letters indicate that the settlement of her estate and his inheritance were not finalized until May 1954. He and Margerie then had an adequate income, but they were never to have enough money to buy a home of their own.

They did come to have a number of friends and many literary acquaintances in the Vancouver area. Some of their closer friends, such as Charles Stansfeld-Jones and Einar and Muriel Neilson, have died and their recollections are lost. What follows are glimpses of Lowry from those Vancouver friends who could be located and who were willing to be interviewed. These recollections are as varied as Lowry's personality and focus on different aspects of his character and his life in the Vancouver area. The passage of time has sometimes dimmed, sometimes sharpened these memories, but Lowry the man and Lowry the artist remain unforgettable — both powerful, both an enigma.

"They Were Like Two Young Lovers"

In the spring of 1940 the Lowrys found lodgings on West 11th Avenue in the home of a Vancouver building contractor, J.D. Smith. The accommodation was comfortable and quiet; life in Vancouver became more tolerable. Lowry completed the third draft of *Under the Volcano* and in August he and Margerie rented a squatter's shack near Roche Point on Burrard Inlet (Map 3).

Six years later the eviction of the Dollarton squatters seemed imminent. In a search for a new home the Lowrys travelled to Vancouver Island (Map 4). The Smiths' daughter, Angela, was married to a Nanaimo restauranteur, Alfred McKee, and the Lowrys decided to visit them at their cottage on Gabriola Island. Although they considered moving to Gabriola, the Lowrys were only there once. They returned to Dollarton to find that the squatters had been given a reprieve, and in January 1947 they left

Angela (Smith) McKee in front of her parents' home on West 11th Avenue in Vancouver, where the Lowrys lived in the spring of 1940. (Courtesy of Alfred McKee.)

Vancouver for a trip to New Orleans, Haiti, and New York, where Lowry took part in book promotions for *Under the Volcano*.

To reach Gabriola the Lowrys had to take a small privately operated ferry called the *Atrevida*. As pointed out by Alfred McKee, the ferry could hold "three cars with a tight squeeze," and also carried foot passengers.[3] After a twenty minute ride the

The Atrevida *docked on Gabriola Island. (Circa 1940. Nanaimo Centennial Museum Q3 – 123.)*

Anderson Lodge on Gabriola Island where the Lowrys stayed for three or four days in October 1946. (Circa 1948. Courtesy of Ruth Darling.)

Lowrys reached Gabriola, where they took the Island's taxi to Anderson Lodge, close to the McKees'. According to Mrs. Ruth Darling, who bought the Anderson Lodge in 1948, the place had summer tenting facilities but the "lodge" was just a family home with one or two spare bedrooms.[4] The Lowrys boarded with the Anderson family for three to four days and visited with the McKees frequently.

This trip in October 1946 became the basis for Lowry's posthumously published novel *October Ferry to Gabriola*. Lowry incorporated local sites into the book: in Nanaimo, a part of the downtown section that included the war memorial known as the Bastion, the Hotel Plaza (Lowry called it the "Ocean Spray"), the Esquire Coffee Shop (from which Lowry quoted menu items), and the dock for the Gabriola ferry (Map 5); from the ferry he saw Newcastle Island and Gallows Point (Lowry called it Hangman's Point) on Protection Island (Map 5); on Gabriola, the Anderson Lodge and the Trenton Rest Home (Lowry called it the Gabriola Rest Home — Map 6). Angela McKee was the model for Angela D'Arrivee, a school teacher on the Canadian prairies. A reference in the novel to a petition for electricity that none of the residents of Gabriola had signed was probably based on Lowry's observations

Panorama of Nanaimo showing the "Ocean Spray" Hotel. The ferry to Gabriola, the Atrevida, *was "just behind the Bastion." (Circa 1940. Nanaimo Centennial Museum, #B – 27.)*

and detailed note taking. According to Alfred McKee, there was such a petition and few Gabriolans signed it as they were reluctant to pay for electricity.

Alfred McKee only met the Lowrys on their one visit to Gabriola Island. He liked them immensely, and the McKees and the Lowrys corresponded for many years. Unfortunately, none of their correspondence has survived. In the 1940s and 1950s Gabriola was a beautiful, secluded spot and McKee remembers that "the trees hung cathedral-like over the road"; he feels it would have been an ideal spot for Malcolm and Margerie. The following recollections were recorded in an interview with Alfred McKee, on Gabriola Island, in January 1985:

> In the spring of 1940 the Lowrys were looking for a place to live and a mutual friend advised them to go and see Mr. and Mrs. J.D. Smith, my mother and father-in-law. They lived on Eleventh Avenue, about three blocks east of Granville Street in the residential area known as Fairview. The Smiths had some spare rooms because their daughter Angela had gone to the prairies to work as a nurse. They were lonely and missing Angela, so when the Lowrys arrived at the house asking if the Smiths would be interested in renting out some rooms, Mrs. Smith said they would love to have them. Malcolm and Margerie lived there for several months.
>
> If I remember correctly the Lowrys had their own bedroom and Angela's mother gave them free access to the kitchen. I think Malcolm and Margerie felt at home there, and from what Angela told me, Margerie was taking Angela's place: Margerie was just like a daughter to them. Mrs. Smith wrote Angela every week telling her about the Lowrys and what wonderful people they were. The Smiths knew that Malcolm was a writer...but didn't ask many questions about the Lowrys' circumstances. They asked the Smiths not to say anything about them should there be any enquiries. They didn't want anyone to know where they were. I think Malcolm was trying to get away from his old cronies so he and Margerie could make a go of it....[5] The Smiths enjoyed them as friends.
>
> In October 1946 they came to Gabriola Island to visit Angela and myself but they didn't tell us they were coming. Travelling home on the ferry I saw this young couple who were so excited, running all around the ferry: above on the upper deck, back down again and all around. The woman was dressed in a beautiful fur coat. I didn't know who they were and when I got home I told Angela about this young couple on the ferry who were so excitedly observing and taking in everything. They didn't miss a thing.
>
> The Lowrys arrived on the Island in the afternoon and took the taxi to Anderson Lodge, now called Surf Lodge, which was about a mile

Malcolm Lowry on board the ferry to Gabriola, the Atrevida, *in October 1946. (Special Collections Library, U.B.C., BC 1614/15.)*

from our cabin. Later on that evening they arrived at our house, having walked down from the Lodge. We didn't have electricity, at that time it was all coal oil lamps, and it was pitch dark outside. I heard this "knock knock knock" on the veranda. I opened the door, looked out at the pitch dark, and heard a woman's voice say "Hello Angela." I immediately said, "Come in." As soon as they came into the light I recognized them as the couple that I had seen on the ferry; especially when I saw the fur coat. I found out later that Margerie had just received some money from a book that she had written, some royalties, so she really "blew herself" on the coat, as she put it.

48

We had a wonderful evening together talking about their travel experiences and life in Dollarton, which they really loved. Malcolm told us how he would jump off the veranda into the water. He loved swimming and thought that was ideal. We also talked about music, the arts, and Margerie's career as an actress in silent films. And Malcolm spoke about going to Cambridge and his experience at sea, which he said was quite an education. He spoke of the different people and characteristics of Mexico and also discussed some of his experiences there. He told one story about the living accommodations. Where he was staying there was a courtyard which the living quarters looked onto. Angela said that sounded very nice. Malcolm had quite a sense of humour and he said, "Oh it was wonderful, especially the plumbing. In the toilet facilities the water container was up on the wall with a chain, and to flush the toilet you pulled this chain. However you were never sure if it was going to flush the toilet or give you a shower bath. Other than that it was quite comfortable."

During their stay we discussed Malcolm and Margerie's writings. They said they'd lost a lot of their manuscripts in the fire that destroyed their shack. Margerie and Malcolm both said that they were fortunate in having saved some of the manuscripts and that they would just have to rewrite the ones that were lost.

The next evening we went over onto the bluff [Map 6]. Even though it was October it was a beautiful warm evening. Margerie was very much interested in the stars and heavenly bodies and told us that she had ground her own telescope lens. We all laid there on the bluff, looking up in the clear sky, and she told us all about the various constellations. It was most interesting. Malcolm had a great smile upon his face; great pride in her knowing all this. Angela said to me afterwards, "You know they're just like a couple of kids. It's as if they've just fallen in love."

While they were here they went for walks around this area, but not down to the south end of the Island. Malcolm was very observant and he was intrigued with the stone formation down at the bluff. The water had cut in on the bank so it was honeycombed, as it still is, and very beautiful.

Malcolm and Margerie fell in love with Gabriola and expressed a desire to come back. At the time we thought they might move here. It would have been an ideal spot for them, and Angela said we would try to make some arrangements to get them here. There was a businessman in Vancouver, a Mr. Vag Marsh, who had a lot of property on Gabriola Island. He had a place down the road from us, on the waterfront, and often spent his summers there. We told him about Malcolm and Margerie and that we'd like to find a place for them. Mr. Marsh said, "You've found a place for them. They can have my place." Mr. Marsh was a writer in his own right, and was very interested in meeting and getting to know the Lowrys. Unfortunately, he never did.

Berry Point Road on Gabriola Island, close to the cabin that was offered to the Lowrys. (Circa 1946. Courtesy of Alfred McKee.)

They did talk of moving to Gabriola but then Malcolm had to travel regarding his book [*Under the Volcano*].... They sent postcards and letters telling us about the trip, how Malcolm was being received, and about getting royalties. I remember on one postcard he wrote, "They talk about the Blue Danube, it doesn't compare with the waters of Gabriola. It is so much nicer on Gabriola than here."

Malcolm did not drink while they were here and we had a pleasant time together. Before they caught the ferry back to Vancouver they came in and had dinner in my restaurant in Nanaimo [Esquire Coffee Shop, 42 Commercial Street – Map 6]. I was so glad to see them again before they left. To me they were extroverts. They just gave of themselves. They were glad to discuss anything and were keenly interested in things around them, no matter what it was. They were just out to observe and learn. They were so happy together; they were like two young lovers, just full of ginger. After they had gone, some of the people in the restaurant remarked that they seemed like jolly folks. It's too bad they never did move here. I would have enjoyed getting to know them better and would have considered them among my friends.

In 1946 the McKees lived in Nanaimo and had a cottage on Gabriola; they later expanded the cottage into a house and became full-time residents of the Island. Alfred McKee is retired and still lives on Gabriola Island, in the same location the Lowrys visited. Unfortunately, Angela McKee passed away a year before this interview was conducted; according to Alfred, she knew much more than he about the Lowrys, particularly their relationship with the Smiths.

"Life Was Always Dramatic When the Lowrys Were Around"

As with all of the Lowrys' Vancouver friends, Marjorie and Downie Kirk did not see them regularly: the demands of writing, and the long journey to and from Vancouver kept the Lowrys isolated. The couples would see each other during the Kirks' periodic visits to Dollarton in the summer, when they vacationed in their beach shack, and the Lowrys attended occasional parties hosted by the Kirks in their Vancouver home.

Marjorie Kirk did not feel as close to the Lowrys as her father (Jimmy Craige) or her husband did. She found the relationship strained by Lowry's drinking, and thought his resulting behaviour "pitiful."

From an interview conducted in March 1985 Marjorie Kirk recalls:

We came to know the Lowrys when they lost their house to a fire in 1944. They felt really bad about that fire; it was a painful loss to them. Malcolm always said that Margerie saved everything but one manuscript. My dad offered them our shack to stay in because we only used it in the summertime. They used it for a few weeks.

The first time we met them we were visiting my mother. Malcolm and Margerie came over to thank us for letting them stay in our place. Malcolm had a few drinks to bolster his courage before he came over and he was a little incomprehensible. He had enjoyed reading the collection of old magazines we had in our shack and thought Downie must be his kind of person because he saved all these magazines. Shortly after that he brought us the first four chapters of *Under the Volcano*.

Downie really loved Malcolm. He thought Malcolm was a great person, was very impressed with his sense of humour, and got a lot of enjoyment out of his company. My husband was a scholarly sort of person, and he and Malcolm both loved ideas and literature. Malcolm would ask Downie how certain things were said or spelled in various languages and that was right along Downie's alley. Apart from that, they were just two human beings who liked each other. They were both fond of jazz but I didn't really know too much about Malcolm's musical interests. He used to spread his fingers, fall on the piano, and play a few chords. Everybody would say, "Oh, Ooh," but to me it just sounded like someone playing in drunkenness. We weren't always in Dollarton when the Lowrys were. Actually we did more visiting with them in our Vancouver home. Life was always dramatic when the Lowrys were around: like the time Malcolm fell into the sewer. He went out to say goodbye to somebody who had been at the party we were having, and he didn't come back. We couldn't believe that he'd gone off with them. Downie finally went out to look for him and found him lying in the sewer ditch that ran along the front of the house. I don't know whether he was happily lying in the ditch, but he didn't make any outcries. He had to be fished out and cleaned up. He was quite pitiful at times.

Many of the friends who came to our parties enjoyed Malcolm. One of these friends was Dunc Murray. Dunc did not have much education but he was very intellectual and leftist in his views. He was fond of poetry, a great lover of Keats, and could quote reams of poetry. He was an elderly person by the time he got to know the Lowrys. Dunc liked a drink or two or three or four, and he enjoyed the Lowrys' company very much; they enjoyed his too.

Malcolm liked to have a bit to drink: he needed oiling with some because he was uncomfortable otherwise. He could be extremely pleasant and good company as long as he didn't drink too much, which wasn't usually the case. He was also very good to converse with when he'd had a small amount to drink, but after he'd had too much one would lose contact with him. Malcolm would separate himself and, although physically present, he would no longer be a part of the gathering: he'd be on another plane of thought; his conversations would become monologues; if one tried to have a discussion with him one couldn't always keep the connection because his mind would jump and the conversation would become bewildering.

As far as I was concerned he became a little unpleasant when he had too much to drink. He would fall down in the living room, pass out, and burn cigarette holes in the rug. He didn't believe in moderation and that's one thing he and my husband would disagree on. One morning around 3:00 or 4:00, Downie suggested we call it an evening. Malcolm said something like, "You'll wish you hadn't said that." He didn't ever want to stop once he got going.

It's probably true that Malcolm was sensitive about his own feelings, but I don't think he was too sensitive about how anybody else was feeling. He wasn't terribly thoughtful about others, though he could be very apologetic when he realized he had done or said something he shouldn't have. Although he could swim really well he seemed to feel that he had some physical incompetence. I don't know whether it was imaginary, but we did hear hints of him having been physically incompetent as a young person: something to do with the trouble he had with his eyesight. Malcolm also seemed to feel that he had been badly treated by his mother and his father, that he didn't get the love he should have. I wondered whether these feelings were just a result of oversensitivity, or if his drinking was the problem.

He was childish in that there were things he didn't want to do himself, and he often seemed to think he should be waited on. One time he fell off our wharf in Dollarton and that was very strange: he was wading in water that was up to his knees and he held out his hand for me to pull him up onto the float. He was heavy and I knew I couldn't pull him up, he would pull me down if I tried. He was only in a foot and a half of water so I told him to just walk ashore. He was a bit miffed with me for that. He really figured I should have pulled him out.

The local people thought the Lowrys were crazy because they didn't fit any pattern — they were different. Some people found them exciting and interesting for that reason, but most people wondered what was wrong with them. Most of the people in the shacks just came for a little holiday and didn't get to know the people who lived there all year long. We wouldn't have come to know the Lowrys that well ourselves if they hadn't stayed in our place.

You had to have lived on the Dollarton beach to really know what it was like. It was not everybody's cup of tea. Some people found it difficult to live there because of the physical hardships: lack of water, lack of electricity, lack of plumbing. In the summer the Dollarton beach was pleasant; in the winter it was quite different. The hardships didn't seem to bother the Lowrys, but I think Margerie would probably have liked a few more comforts. She waited on Malcolm, so he didn't feel the discomforts as much. He would live in his head but she had to be the practical one and had to worry about and cope with the problems.

Malcolm loved the beach and I don't think he ever wanted to leave it. They left Dollarton in 1954, but Malcolm always said he would return. We had the feeling that Margerie didn't intend to come back, that she wanted a more comfortable life. I haven't looked at Malcolm's letters for a long time, but after they left I think his mood was quite despondent.

When we heard of his death I don't think anybody was really surprised because he wasn't a person who took the best care of himself. But it was very sad. Downie felt very bad.

"Happy Times Together"

Downie Kirk saw the Lowrys more frequently in the summer months, when his family would vacation in Dollarton. They would spend time basking in the sun, sipping gin, swimming in the refreshing waters of Burrard Inlet, participating in "talk fests," and listening to Malcolm and Margerie read from their writings.

Kirk and Lowry had a camaraderie based on affection and humour, as well as shared interests in literature, music, art, philosophy, politics, thought transference, and mysticism. A language teacher in a Vancouver high school, Kirk's linguistic abilities were often helpful to Lowry, as he liked to incorporate foreign words into his writings for dramatic effect and emphasis. In the late 1940s and early 1950s, Lowry also had a large volume of foreign correspondence that was related to various translations of *Under the Volcano*; Kirk often interpreted these letters for Lowry.

Kirk wrote and published one article about his friend, "More Than Music: The Critic as Correspondent," in which he discussed aspects of Lowry's personality revealed through his letters.[6] Kirk died in 1964, before he or anyone else had recorded his personal reminiscences of Lowry. What has survived is the correspondence between the two, conveying the depth and warmth of the relationship. Their letters speak for both men:

Oct. 23, 1948

Dear Malcolm,

Many times before today I have thought of writing a letter to you and Margerie to hear how you have been enjoying your stay in Europe. . . . I had hoped. . .that you would return to your hideout on the Inlet this summer. . . . Yesterday [while reading]. . .I was. . .transported back to the time of our first real literary association—the evening that old Dunc, you and I discussed in the inlet shack so many interesting problems of art. . . . Last spring Margerie's book *Horse in the Sky* circulated among our reading friends. . .and [all] were very much impressed by Margerie's first attempt at serious fiction. . . . Have you been working. . .on a novel of the stature of *Under the Volcano*?. . . . Recently [I read about] *The Book of Canadian Poetry*, edited by A.J.M. Smith, [and] read that the last part is devoted to the works of modern poets & includes poems by B.C.'s leading poets. I am looking forward to getting a copy so that I may read some of *your* poems; I have not forgotten the unusual pleasure I received when I heard the author himself read "Sestina in a Cantina"....Have you made any definite plans about return[ing] to *Dollarton*? I have two books of *yours — The Castle* (Kafka), *The Hidden Damage* (Stern)....Shall I simply hold these till I hear from you?

Needless to say, we have missed you both terribly and I can hardly wait to hear your first hand account of the island of Capri....We must have many an evening together when you get back.

Arrivederci,
Downie (U.B.C. 1:33)

Sunday, March 20/49

Dear Malcolm:

Now that the *Ides of March* have come and gone, perhaps it will be quite safe for me to write to you again without experiencing another of those extraordinary coincidences, for I also felt that there was something mysterious or, as you say, telepathic about the way our communications were carried on *last week*....I was really thrilled to get your letter: I thought, at first that it was a reply to mine, but of course that was out of the question. I sat right down and made a translation of the Italian letter, a very pleasant task for me. As I had just spent a year writing a diary in Italian, it was interesting to see what sort of job I could make of it. I have purposely made it very literal...so that you can go over it again in the original and get the Italian flavour....Today Marjorie and I heard four Beethoven Symphonies: 4th & 7th over the radio with...the New York Philharmonic; 1st & 9th here in Vancouver...with Jacques Singer conducting the Vancouver Symphony....On two occasions today I had very definite thoughts about you....When you get this letter, perhaps you will discover more telepathy at work — that is, if you did not undergo that telepathectomy you mentioned in your last letter....The Canadian commentator said about Beethoven's 7th that the composer built it to last and not to catch a fashion; I immediately thought of those ten years of your labour over the *Volcano*. This afternoon, as I watched Jacques Singer conduct, I thought how much his artistic endeavors resembled yours. If you have not already met him you'll have to do so, for I'm sure you'll like him....I do hope that your operation was very successful and that you are well on the way to recovering that robust health of yours by the time this letter reaches you. You should be in best of shape this summer with lots of swimming practice: we may even swim the inlet together — something I have planned to do for years.[7]

Yours ever,
Downie (U.B.C. 1:33)

55

[Spring, 1949]

Dear Downie:

A thousand thanks for the translation and the letter.... Meanwhile here is the Marcelin, in English that leaves much to be desired, in our opinion, though it is extremely funny in places.... It is not about Voodoo, chiefly, but witchcraft: there is a difference, perhaps not apparent to the layman. Still it is worth reading. (Warning — it is incredibly obscene in places too so don't leave it on the piano.)... Both our loves to yourself and Marjorie and Dorothy [Kirk's daughter].

Malcolm
(Selected Letters, 175)

October 1, 1949

Dear Malcolm,

As Marjorie and I are planning a little party for Friday night, Oct. 7th, at our house, we should like very much to have you and Margery [sic] with us that evening, if you have not already planned something else and that injured back of yours is well enough to permit you to make the trip. You could, of course, plan on staying over night with us, and make the return trip to Dollarton at your leisure. I expect the party will get underway between 8 or 9 in the evening. Incidentally, I hope you will not feel obliged to bring any liquid refreshment, as I hope to have plenty for all to get *perfectamente borracho*, if they so desire. *Positivamente!*

There are a number of matters that I should like to talk over with you. In the first place, I have just got home from Mt. St. Joseph's Hospital — a Roman Catholic institution.... I had a run-in with a screwball, incompetent, sadistic orderly and I should like to compare notes with you, as I know that you had a pretty trying experience at St. Paul's Hospital with the orderlies there.... By the way, I read some passages from the *Volcano* to the patients and nurses in my ward and I know that they were much appreciated. I reread to myself one morning around dawn the last chapter of the book and found it more powerful than ever before: I must have been [in] a more sensitive mood than usual!... I am enclosing the snapshot that was taken beside your cabin on August 26th. Everybody seems to be agreed that you took a *particularly* good picture.... I shall never forget your going in for a plunge "harness on back"; the glorious weather — particularly the blue water and the blue sky... our looking at the proofs in French of

56

Under the Volcano, Margery [sic] serving nonchalantly the drinks and wondering about the exact spot in Keats' poetry where the phrase *Tender is the Night* occurs; Dunc Murray reciting to Mrs. Limpus, while you were drying yourself in the shack, whole verses from *Ode To Melancholy*; the kids rowing by in Jim's rowboat wondering about the strange activities of the adults on the shore. . . . If I could only write, it would be the sort of situation I should like to describe with all its contours, tones & implications. . . .

> Yours affectionately,
> Downie (U.B.C. 1:33)

[Early October, 1949]

Dear Downie:

Thanks very much for your letter and for the invitation. . . . We'd awfully much like to come but since correspondence between us at this short distance seems to take rather longer than it used to traverse the

Friends visiting at the Lowrys' shack, August 26, 1949. Lowry is standing, wearing a backbrace. Left to right are Dorothy Limpus, Dunc Murray, Downie Kirk, George Limpus. (Courtesy of Jean Craig.)

Roman Empire is it too much to leave it open? We are working hard on a movie treatment and whether we can come rather depends on how much work we have completed by then; at the moment it looks favourable, but we may run into a snag, and it seems rather important that we finish it *quam celerime*, if not indeed *sine mora*.[8] At first I thought I couldn't come because I could scarcely bring my fracture board with me;[9] now it occurs to me I could sleep on the floor. *Is it too much to ask for a bit of floor?* (It would not — er — be the first time that I have done that.)... I'm glad you're better now after your operation — the combination of a haemorrhoidectomy with a Catholic institution sounds sadistic enough, without the orderly, in all conscience. It sounds a dreadful experience. I'm touched at your reading the *Volcano* to your fellow-suffers — if you want to make people feel real cheery you might find Maxim Gorky's *The Lower Depths* even more helpful.... We saved a grebe. And the world progresses....

Love,
Malcolm
(Selected Letters, 181 – 183)

Dollarton
[January, 1950]

Dear Downie:

This is a letter of thanks to you and Marjorie for a wonderful evening but also a letter of apology so it is addressed to you alone, since I do not feel even worthy of addressing your wife at the moment.

My Margerie has impressed me with my bad behavior but I can't very well write a letter of apology to her either and as for the behavior I can only hope that it does not seem so bad to you as it does to me.

I am also told I used bad language in front of your wife and Dorothy; this is utterly inexcusable of course — nor is it an excuse when I say that I would not have done so had I been aware of their presence. But I was not so aware and here you must believe me. I am deeply sorry.

That there are reasons for all this, such as that I must have had one too many phenobarbital (My faithful enemy Phenobarbas — treacherous to the last), or that I felt myself in some way frustrated — apparently a nearly total illusion — in my conversation with Les [Downie's brother], that I was, or rather became — and in what a damned mean manner also — *borracho*, etc., are not proffered as excuses, but are merely set down in an unsuccessful attempt to make me feel better.... My mood... is pretty grim. I would say it was totally grim—for I count it a failure in character if I of all people (because God knows my work should give me sufficient practice) can't keep my wretched Id in order for five minutes.

All I can say is that I hope your wife and you will forgive me. Though frankly I see no reason why you should. Nor why, should I say that I can at least see it won't happen again, I should even be given the opportunity. . . . I would ask you though if you can—since it is the New Year—to put the whole thing out of your minds, hearts, and speech: expunge it as a wretched aberration for which I hope I can make amends.

Sincerely
Malcolm
(Selected Letters, 189-190)

Dollarton
March 2, 1950

Dear old Downie:

Don't forgive me for not writing—do certainly though, the reason is I'm working 17 hours a day against time, and couldn't write, not even you—but will you please for my sake take your Greek cap off the hook, put on your gaff-topsail boots, your hood, assemble your bow of burning gold and take a flying leap into your desk, what time the gramaphone is playing the record about the antiquated old antique, repay my bad behavior by answering as soon as you conceivably can the following antiquated old antique and learned questions? What I want mainly are the names of two Greek ships, and one Greek town, in Greek capitals: the first ship ARISTOTLE, the second ship OEDIPUS TYRANNUS, the town ANTIPOLIS. The difference is that both of the names of the ships should be in modern Greek characters—capitals— the town in ancient Greek capitals—I don't think there is any difference, is there? But Aristotle in Greek ancient or modern would be Aristotelis, would it not? And Oedipus Tyrannus sounds like a Roman version and would not be Oedipus Tyrannus in Greek? Be that as it may, they both have to be translated visually in the work in question into ARISTOTLE and OEDIPUS TYRANNUS but I want them visually in Greek capital letters first for dramatic effect. . . . The thing is it comes at a dramatic and important point in the work as we are presenting it; it isn't a question of showing off knowledge I don't possess, but I don't want to make too naïve a mistake right off. . . . Finally, I thought you'd be tickled to know, the *Volcano* has made a hit in France, where it is coming out three times in the next months: first in a classic series, then Correa, and it is also being serialized in the Paris daily newspaper *Combat*! They have decided that it is the writing on the wall, that your amigo is everything from the *Four Quartets* (which he has never read) to Joyce (whom he

59

dislikes) — finally related him to the Jewish prophetic Zohar (of which he knows nothing — they have some other comments to make too, about Macbeth, but that is nothing to what someone is just going to say in Victoria, over the C.B.C., where they have decided that the Consul is really Moby Dick masquerading as the unconscious aspect of the Cadbosaurus in the Book of Jonah, or words to that effect.

I am going to present you with a copy of the French translation and we should have some fun out of it when you have glozed upon it.

For the rest, we have many of your books, kindly lent at your and Marjorie's good party never-to-be-forgotten. Of them I have read backwards and forwards the excellent *Concert Companion*, which has taught me a great deal about writing (I mean from the form of music... [and] it also helped me to begin to understand music a bit better). Our friend Cecil Gray makes some rather good remarks therein — and I'm glad you liked his book — more of that later. Shean on Gandhi is interesting and important in substance... but it doesn't seem quite as absorbing as his other books, though you may find it more so. Merton on monasteries contains some phenomenal coincidences and parallels of some interest philosophically which I would like to discuss next time we meet.... It is a paradox in its own terms. How the hell can a writer go into a monastery and go on writing books and then pretend he's given up "everything," I ask you, isn't he a sort of Trappist monk to start with? That a monastery might, in essence, be the capital of the world at this juncture is a possibility which not even Nietzsche were he alive would care to question — or would he? Anyhow, it is a good idea — or is it?

I have some other funny and even dramatic things to say but will close now, merely intimating that it be understood how fine it will be to see you all again, asking your indulgence for my having suddenly persecuted you with so many questions, adding my hope that you will answer them too, and to that all our very best wishes to the three of you, also imagining that when Dorothy has not been playing the tune about the antiquated old antique on the gramophone, she will have been playing even better tunes of her own upon the more modern and sober — or at any rate upright — piano....

Malcolm
(Selected Letters, 193 – 197)

March 8, 1950.

Dear Malcolm,

Friday afternoon, on the way home from school, I dropped into the Public Library to pick up a copy of *The Letters and Treatises of Cicero & Pliny*...ran into my brother Leslie,...started drinking beer with him in the Broadway Hotel, met an old friend of his — a salesman who sells automatic machines for washing beer glasses to the big hotels, went on a spree "leaving my necktie God knows where," and didn't get home till early morning. Instead of bouncing a rolling pin off my head, Marjorie handed me your letters, and I was in such a state of inebriation that all I remember of that moment is the delightful sensation I had of ploughing through prose sprinkled à la James Joyce with Latin, French and German — and Greek characters dancing before my eyes! The music of the names *Aristotle*, *Oedipus Tyrannus*, *Antipolis*, was like that of a bell tolling me back to Temple or some other beautiful vale in Thessaly. It wasn't till the next morning that I got the rude shock that there were some questions in that letter which were to be answered. . . . I enjoyed your comments no-end on the books you borrowed last fall. . . . On the matter of the Greek spellings you are absolutely correct about the ancient spelling of Aristotle, the Latin version of *Oedipus*, and the fact that there is no difference between the modern and ancient Greek characters. . . . I have printed the spellings of the Greek names on a separate piece of paper. . . . I should like to read Aristotle and Plato in the original to build up some philosophical armour against the H. Bomb. . . . The developments and tensions over the H. Bomb seem to be taking place around us at such a terrific speed that I doubt seriously whether I'll have time to brush up my Greek before the annihilation begins! . . . As Schiller has Talbot say in *Du Jungfrau von Orléans*:

> Unsinn, du siegst, und ich muss untergehen!
> Mit der Dummheit Kämpfen Götter selbst vergebens.

I've heard you comment on human folly in similar terms. . . . I am planning a musical evening for Easter, at which time I hope you and Margerie will be able to come down and stay over night with us — that is, provided you can get away from the busy task of writing.

Yours truly,
Downie

P.S. Marjorie & Dorothy send their very best wishes to you both. Dorothy, in particular, has been pestering me about a trip to camp [Dollarton] and will no doubt want to come over and see you when we pay our long delayed visit to the beach (U.B.C. 1:33).

(Postmarked Dec. 13, 1950)

Dear Downie,

It was wonderful seeing you the other night. . . . We're very relieved that Mrs. Craig is well recovered: conversely, and at about the same time, I lost my own mother. . . . This threw me emotionally out of gear somewhat; it is hard to say exactly what happens to one on such an occasion even if it doesn't show outwardly: it seems probable that one undergoes spiritually some kind of insurrection, as between the deathward wish that unconsciously wishes to follow one's mother into the grave, and the lifeward one that is striving once more within the conditions of birth itself, towards a rebirth. Such a phenomenon also seems to be occurring in the world outside us, and grim though the picture seems, it doesn't seem half so hopeless as it did in 1939 — or even 1938. Even if communism were temporarily victorious it doesn't carry with it such a hopeless *teleology* of tyranny — even if tyrannical in its present phase — as did Nazism. In short anything [that] is a revolution must keep moving or it doesn't revolute: by its very nature it contains within it the seeds of its own destruction, so by 1989, say, everything ought to be hunky dory, all of which certainly doesn't make it any easier to live in 1950. And it is tragic that the few really selfless men in world affairs, such as Nehru, seem to gain so little hearing. . . . Sometimes I get the impression that not even the people who are actually in the process of making history know in the least what is *really* going on. Or if they do it seems appalling that they should be in the position that they are. . . . We went to see the old silent film *Intolerance* — played straight through without any music at all — a great mistake, since Griffith wrote his own score. . . . I have a lot more to say but will keep it till we meet again, which I hope will be soon. . . .

Cheerio
Malcolm (U.B.C. 2:16)

January 20, 1951

Dear Malcolm:

It was a real delight to hear from you after that wild escapade of mine the other night. I thought I had disgraced myself permanently with you and particularly with Margerie, after so rudely pounding on your door & barging into Margerie's boudoir (Mozart could elaborate on that) in a drunken stupor at three o'clock in the morning! But I guess that sort of thing happens occasionally in the best of regulated families. When Dunc, Leslie and I get *perfectamente borracho* — or even long before we reach that blissful state — we usually talk about looking you up. The other night I guess we just figured the evening would not be complete without a visit with you. Please make apologies to Margerie & tell her that when we drop in again, I shall do my level best to see that it is a more reasonable hour and if possible with some sort of warning of what is impending! . . . I have to send my French

62

papers...off on the 27th and [will] celebrate on the evening of the 28th. If you can make it on that date, I shall be overjoyed see you....I want to hear those *Jazz Classics* again...*Heavy Traffic on Canal Street* and *Biederbecke's composition*....Here's hoping you can make it next week.

Cheerio,
Downie (U.B.C. 1:33)

April, 1951

Dear Malcolm:

Since the beginning of the Easter vacation I have been sick with a very *bad cold*....I had hoped to see you and Margerie this week, but I think...that it will be wise for me to...come on some fine, warm *week-end* a little later in the spring. We shall be able to sit out in the *sun* beside your place and talk things over. I'm looking forward *to that* very much — more than you probably realize. Some of the happiest & most memorable moments that I have spent during the last few summers at Dollarton have been with you and Margerie basking in the sun and chatting, hour after hour. A couple of lines from William Johnson Cory's paraphrase of *Heraclitus*, by Callimachus, keep recurring to me as I think of those happy times we have had together — and which we shall, I hope, have again in goodly number: "I wept, as I remembered, how often you and I / Had tried the sun with talking and sent him down to sky"....I hope to hear from you again soon and better still I hope to get up to see you both before long. I shall drop you a line ahead of time to make sure it's convenient for you. The visit will be for me a tonic of which my spiritual health is in dire need. Till I see you again,

love from All of us.

Yours sincerely,
Downie (U.B.C. 1:33)

Sept. 10/1955

Dear Malcolm & Margerie:

This is a very short note simply to say that I have been thinking of you constantly....After the summer session at U.B.C. finished, Marjorie, Dorothy, Katie [the Kirk's second child, a baby at this time] and I spent a week at Dollarton: we lived at Bill and Jean's [Craig's] place [on Dollarton Highway], but went down everyday to the beach. . . . One day Dorothy (13 years old now) swam across the inlet in *43 minutes.* I decided to swim back and did it in 30 minutes. Naturally I thought about the times that we planned to swim it together. If you ever return, we shall still make that swim. I spent the afternoon of the big swim in your house on the beach talking to Harvey who had helped old Jim in the morning saw up a huge log for firewood.[10] We talked about Summer School, Europe, you and Margerie, *Under the Volcano,* etc.: it was like old times, except that you were missing! . . .

Sincerely,
Downie (U.B.C. 1:33)

Dorothy Kirk swimming in front of her parents' shack. (Courtesy of Jean Craig.)

February 1/57

Dear Malcolm & Margerie:

It's hard to believe that a whole month has slipped away since the beginning of the New Year. I had hoped to answer your Christmas greetings long before this, but... I have neglected my correspondence. We were very glad to hear from you at Christmas & to learn that you are both well. It was grand to hear that you are working like mad on a new novel *October Ferry to Gabriola*. I recall very well you reading to my Marjorie and me the original short story in the beach house at Dollarton. I thought your descriptions of Nanaimo & Gabriola extraordinarily good and... the difficult problem of finding a suitable home particularly well done. As I remember, the story had a touch of universality about it that should make a very wide appeal. I hope in the new work you have maintained that rigorous selection of detail that is obvious in the *Volcano*....Curt Lang and Al Purdy are living in Montreal....I have just written to them to say that you have not forgotten them — those "*wild & memorable* poets"....We all miss *you* here very much. I do hope you & Margerie will be able to make a *triumphant* return to these parts. There has been a literary slump around here since you left....Hoping to hear from you soon or better to see you both before long....This weekend I reread Sartre's *Les jeux sont faits* & Camus' *L'Étranger*...: they remind [me] very much of Malraux, Kafka and yourself. By the way, one of the first words you spoke to me down on the beach were: "Have you read *The Castle*?"....

Yours sincerely,
Downie (U.B.C. 1:33)

Downie Kirk (1910–1964) graduated from the University of B.C. with a Bachelor of Arts and the "French Government Medal"; a Master of Arts; and a teaching certificate. He worked as a high school language instructor in Vancouver. Marjorie Kirk (b. 1912) returned to teaching kindergarten after her husband died. She is now retired and lives with her daughter Katie and family. Marjorie devotes her time to her four granddaughters and the *Voice of Women*, of which she is an active member. The Kirks' daughter Dorothy is a Spanish instructor at Vancouver's Langara College.

"A Great Writer and the Most Lovable of Men"

The Canadian writer and poet Earle Birney began his nineteen year English professorship at the University of British Columbia in 1946. His reputation as a Canadian poet was firmly established as he had twice received the prestigious Governor General's Award for Poetry—for *David and Other Poems* (1942) and *Now is Time* (1945).

In May 1947 Birney received a letter from Malcolm Lowry stating that Sybil Hutchinson, of the Canadian publishing firm McClelland and Stewart, had suggested that the two men meet. Lowry, whose preferences tended toward drinking establishments, wrote: "Luncheon is not our strong suit and instinct vaguely suggests a pub." He went on to say that he thought the "Ladies and Escorts" section of the Hotel Vancouver might possess "the necessary ambiguities" for a rendezvous (U.B.C. 2:10).

Birney found himself "enormously attracted" to Lowry, and a warm friendship developed between the two men and their wives. They shared interests in literature, film, and the natural environment, with good humour and good times. More importantly, as fellow writers, Birney and Lowry became "compañeros," reading their works to one another and offering each other encouragement and advice.

Lowry had published two novels (*Ultramarine*, 1933; *Under the Volcano*, 1947) but also wanted to publish his poetry. In 1941 his poem, "A Bottle From the Sea," had been accepted by the American magazine *Atlantic Monthly*, but, according to Birney, Lowry had been "desolated to find it had been consigned to the small-print back-page 'Contributors' Club' reserved for amateurs."[11] Lowry sought advice from Birney regarding publication of his growing collection of poetry. Birney, who was the editor of the *Canadian Poetry Magazine* (1946–1948), wanted to publish some of Lowry's poems but, paradoxically, had to "wheedle" them from Lowry for the 1947 September and December issues.[12] As guest editor for the British journal *Outposts*, Birney included Lowry's poem "Sunrise" in the special 1948 issue that was dedicated to Canadian poetry.[13] Birney shared Lowry's poems with other Canadian editors who also published them,[14] thereby making Lowry, according to Birney, "an established 'Canadian poet'."[15]

A letter written to Lowry in October 1947 highlights Birney's regard for Lowry's *Under the Volcano*, the literary relationship of the two men, and the rapport that existed between them. Birney wrote:

Although disappointed, I was quite prepared for not seeing you...on Thursday, what with the bus wayward....I greatly enjoyed your poems...in CV [*Contemporary Verse*]; like good work always, they improve with printing....Brace yourself: I am going to spend most of an hour on *Under the Volcano* in a lecture series....I take four evenings to discuss Conrad's *Lord Jim*, Joyce's *Ulysses*, Woolf's *Mrs. Dalloway* and your novel....This is the sort of thing you will have to get used to (wait till the doctoral theses begin, if they haven't already: "Lowry: The Dollarton Period," or "Meat & Drink in Lowry")....I have been telegraphed by...one of the editors of the projected Toronto magazine, *Here & Now*....He says "We would be grateful if you would contact Malcolm Lowry regarding short stories which by devious sources we hear he has...." I dutifully relay this to you, but also warn you that this mag. can pay only Ten Dollars for a story and that if you published one with them you might lose out on a Thousand Dollar fee from an American mag. (which wanted both Can. & Amer. serial rights....Love from us both....

(Earle Birney Papers, Thomas Fisher Rare Book Library, University of Toronto)

Taken at "Lieben," Bowen Island. Left to right are Reg Watters (Canadian editor and anthologist), Malcolm, Margerie, and Earle Birney. (July 1947. Special Collections Library, U.B.C., BC 1614/25.)

After Lowry's death, Birney's interest in his friend's writings continued. He encouraged Margerie to publish her husband's works posthumously. In September 1957 he wrote:

> Above all I count on you, we all do, to see that everything possible of his is published; I think this is a case where you should not think too precisely on Malcolm's own wishes, for he was surely far too hard on his own work and kept things back that should have been published.
> (Birney Papers, University of Toronto)

Birney collected the manuscripts, correspondence, poetry, and other papers that Lowry's friends had saved from the Dollarton shack. On Birney's suggestion, Margerie sold the papers to the University of British Columbia, giving them permanent residence close to the Dollarton beach that Lowry so loved. In September 1960, after spending a day sorting out the manuscripts, Birney wrote Margerie a moving letter that expresses the esteem he felt for his friend and the complex task of collating the collection:

> You will know better than I whether any of the items are unique. The Bellevue novella MS, for example — has it been published?[16] If not do you have the last draft? Was it finished? I thought it one of the most moving stories I had ever experienced, and looking now at the script the voice and presence of Malcolm is all around me and I am back hearing him read it to us. It has been a harrowing mournful day for me, going through all these shards of a great man — what it must be like for you, poor dear, all these months since he died, years now. I admire you very much for having the heart to come back to his papers and drive through and get these stories into print. I hope you won't flag, so long as there is something still to be rescued. . . . Believe me, it has taken much patience. . . to make head or tail of the wads of stuff, because much of it must have blown around the floor of the shack, was water-stained, frayed, and hopelessly out of order. The paperclips holding sections of things together had often rusted and broken. . . . No doubt a lot has been lost before it got to me, but if anything I have pieced together proves of any help to you I will be more than rewarded. I share your knowledge, however imperfectly in my case, that Malcolm was both a great writer and the most lovable of men. His star is not fading.
> (Birney Papers, University of Toronto)

The following is taken from an interview with Earle Birney in Toronto, May 1985, and from correspondence with Birney:

Malcolm felt that he wanted to be a poet. He'd written a lot of poetry but couldn't get it published. He wanted me to see it and I said certainly. I was curious enough but then I realized that Malcolm was his own Consul: that he was a heavy drinker and there was more than one Malcolm Lowry. He was full of very high and low mood swings which were mainly alcoholic ones. When he was sober and trying to stay sober he was very pessimistic about himself and he wouldn't show me any of his poems. He'd only show a poem to me when he was high and then it wouldn't necessarily be a good poem. Most of the stuff I never saw while he was alive.

Though his chief literary ambition from schooldays onward was to be a poet, Lowry wanted to try everything: short stories, dramas, novels, film scenarios, travel articles, critical essays, sonnets, sestinas, haiku. He was a *writer*. But he was too self-centered, too inexperienced about others, to be contented with prose fiction alone; when he felt most deeply he turned to verse, especially after he came under the influence of Conrad Aiken. Indeed some of the most powerful passages in *Under the Volcano* were first written as verse. By the time he came to Dollarton he had the habit of recording whatever day-to-day experiences most moved him in poetic form, seeing an eagle, finding a strange flower. And later he would re-work some of these poems into the prose of his *Volcano* and his later novels.

After his death Margerie and I sorted out the manuscripts rescued from the shack and worked side by side in dating and cataloguing them. Her help in deciphering his handwriting and in dating was invaluable. Sometimes she could distinguish between earlier and later versions of a poem by recalling when a particular colour of stationery had been bought, or the date of some incident he had developed into a sonnet. Before the summer was out, and she returned to Beverley Hills, we had the possible text for at least eighty percent of the manuscript verse, and the raw material for the bibliography we later printed.[17] We also had a publishable text, made by the interweaving of three separate and incomplete drafts, of a novella, first published in Paris in 1963, called *Lunar Caustic*.

I had also, with Margerie's enthusiastic support, proceeded to place over a hundred of the retrieved poems in thirty or more journals in Canada, the U.S., and England. By 1962 most of these poems had been given a more permanent home by Lawrence Ferlenghetti in his City Lights Books series, which has since gone through a score or more of editions.[18]

But there were still many more Lowry poems lying unknown in manuscript. At Margerie's urgings I eventually set about to prepare an edition of all his publishable verse, under a title Lowry himself had chosen, *The Lighthouse Invites the Storm*. I spent all my spare time from professional duties, for a calendar year, collating, deciphering the multifarious versions, and researching the backgrounds and references to lighten obscurities and provide the best possible texts. My final edition provided a hundred pages tracing the life-story of Lowry as a poet, and another hundred of textual elucidations and alternate readings, as well as more than two hundred pages of Lowry poetry.

When I had it finished I phoned Margerie inviting her to see it. To my astonishment she declined, saying she understood that I had excluded some of Malcolm's poems. I said: "Of course. You and I agreed at the start that some of his poems were incomplete and some, to say the least, derivative, leaving us vulnerable to charges of plagiarism. I did the editing job you agreed on." Margerie replied merely that "every word, every line that Malcolm wrote, has to be published." She then hung up.

The truth is that Malcolm Lowry was given to imitating the literature he admired, sometimes to the point of flagrant borrowings without acknowledgement. Conrad Aiken reproached him for the excessive borrowings of phrases, ideas and attitudes from Aiken's *Blue Voyage* to be found in Lowry's *Ultramarine*. He also, for the same work, borrowed even more extensively from an English translation of Nordahl Grieg's *The Ship Sails On*. Some of these echoings occur also in Lowry's earlier poems. I could not have published many of Lowry's poems without noting these unacknowledged loans, and my notations would need to be so numerous that Lowry's reputation as a writer would suffer a good deal of damage.

Margerie, of course, could publish the poems without my consent but not with my textual notes, alternate readings, editorial apparatus, or my name. However, she chose to do nothing, realizing perhaps that her London publishers had by this time also seen my edition in typescript and were all set to publish it. In such a situation, no other reputable publisher would touch it without my consent. And I could not publish the poems themselves without her consent. Lowry's *Lighthouse* was turned off and has never been re-lit.

The Birneys and the Lowrys saw each other often: both couples belonged to a foreign film society and attended showings at the Varsity Theatre; they also attended a number of the same gatherings. In George Robertson's 1961 two-part C.B.C. television program (*Malcolm Lowry: To the Volcano*; *The Forest Path*), Earle Birney described Lowry's demeanor while drinking.[19] (The following is reprinted with permission from George Robertson.)

When he would be moving from exhilaration into tipsiness and into drunkenness, which was a fairly rapid process...there would be moments...when he would be...at the top of his form verbally and everything that was said, or that he was saying, or that happened, you could feel had suddenly become part of a novel that you were in. The whole room was part of it and everything lost its ordinary reality and took on the reality he was imposing on it. And he would be getting more and more into these complex Jamesian-Joycean sentences...and they would be coming out of him spontaneously...[and] with considerable flow....Then he would get more and more incoherent and less able to control his mind and more and more frustrated at this....He would start some extremely interesting and complex sentence and stop in the middle of it because there was a word he couldn't get....After a while you would start to say something to carry on the conversation and he'd be extremely annoyed....Everyone had to stop until he got this word and got this sentence finished. Then he'd go on to a further stage in which we no longer existed really. He'd needed us as an audience but now he had invented his own audience and hallucination was beginning to take over.... These familiars that he felt were in his life (things invisible to us...animals, grotesque creatures, shapes and spirits of various things) were in and around the corners of the room....He would move over to a corner and sometimes even turn his back on a group and go on with what he was saying, but it would become more and more directed to something in the corner....He was apparently being answered, and corrected, and contradicted by some familiar in the corner of the room. It was sometimes hard to know...to what extent he was play-acting this and to what extent he was caught up in it. There was always...a little period in the middle where you could pull him back by some kind of a joke...but at times he would be so caught up in this he would suffer and...sweat and he would just be torn by the terrible inner drama...[of] fear, guilt, and emotion....Very shortly after that he would pass out, often stiff as a board, on the carpet.

Earle Birney (b. 1904) is a Canadian poet, novelist, and literary critic. He won the Stephen Leacock medal for humour for his novel *Turvey* (1949), and is known for his essays on Chaucerian Irony and for his radio dramas, thirteen of which were produced by the C.B.C. from 1946 to 1957. In 1965 Birney became the Writer in Residence at the University of Toronto, the first person to hold such a position in Canada. He still lives in Toronto and is kept busy writing, as well as giving readings and lectures.

"A Phantasmagoric of Relationships"

Hilda and Phil Thomas were students at the University of British Columbia when they met the Lowrys. They saw them on a couple of occasions at parties hosted by the Birneys. Lowry drank heavily at these gatherings and the Thomases' recollections convey Lowry's behaviour, his intricate thought processes which he often expressed through symbols, and the aura he created. Hilda recalls:

> I was in the first of Earle Birney's Creative Writing classes at U.B.C. He introduced the class to Lowry's *Under the Volcano* and he asked us to write a review of the novel as an assignment. Birney showed all the reviews to Lowry and, I think, as a result of my review, my husband Phil and I were invited out to the Birneys' at Acadia Camp [at U.B.C.], one evening, to meet Lowry.[20]
>
> I recall him standing in the kitchen with a glass full of rum, getting progressively drunker, and talking about the fire department; how it was the most important thing in the world and firemen the most important people.
>
> I also met him in Dollarton. We had a group of amateur or would be writers, under Birney's tutelage, which called itself *Authors Anonymous*. One evening we had a meeting-cum-party at Birney's Dollarton shack. It was a few hundred yards down the beach from the Lowrys' and they were invited. At these get-togethers people would read their writings and there would be criticism. Lowry read "Sestina" and "Seagull" but there was not any criticism of his works as he was a guest reader. It was at this party that Lowry made some complimentary remarks about Norman Newton. He was very young and Lowry considered him to be a very serious writer.
>
> Birney said that Lowry was ill at ease in social situations and as a result would drink, but I think he drank because liquor was available. Lowry was undoubtedly an alcoholic but he may have handled his drinking better in Dollarton as a result of the demands of writing and the isolation. As his letters point out, the liquor laws in B.C. at that time were such that if you ran out of booze you were out of luck for a long time unless you could afford to pay a cab driver to bring out bootleg booze. So he was in a forced state of sobriety for part of the time, but when he went to a party he drank.
>
> When he came to our *Authors Anonymous* party, Lowry wasn't supposed to drink because he had fallen off his wharf, injured his back, and was under a doctor's care. He got into an altercation with a member of the group who taunted him into drinking, and he got quite drunk. He pointed his finger Michelangelo style at the person who had been baiting him and said, "God will—! God will—!" He never said what God would do, but you had a feeling that he knew. It was a part

of his charisma that even his most ambiguous and unfinished utterances seemed to come from some special knowledge.

In the course of that evening I went back to the Lowrys' shack with Margerie, who wanted to see if the fire was still going. We hiked in the dark along the bank up above the shacks because the tide was in. I talked to her while she fed the fire. She and Lowry had just come back from a trip to Europe and she told me about going into the Sistine Chapel with him. Lowry had gone in with his tie undone, his sleeves rolled up, and his coat off. As they were wandering around, Margerie lost sight of him. She couldn't find him so she retraced her steps and found him crouching down behind one of the pews, rolling his sleeves down, doing up his tie and putting on his jacket because he thought that in the presence of such genius he ought to be properly dressed; that it was a discourtesy, almost what amounted to sacrilege, not to be properly dressed in the Sistine Chapel and in the presence of such genius.

We went back to the party, which had turned into a rather unpleasant occasion, to find that most of the others had left. I remember Lowry sitting out on the front porch of Birney's shack singing: "Oh the days of the Kerry dancers, Oh the ring of the piper's tune/ Oh for one of those hours of gladness, Gone alas like our youth too soon." A very appropriate song. Then he looked at Phil, who had Margerie on his knee, and offered her to Phil, saying, "Take her, I have had many children by her."

Lowry was so drunk by this time that he couldn't get home on his own. Birney was exceedingly displeased with the whole evening and refused to have anything to do with helping Lowry, so Phil was elected. Although Phil was big, Lowry was a heavy, barrel-chested man and was quite a weight to handle. I remember watching Phil stagger off with Lowry draped drunkenly across his shoulders and Birney calling after them, "Come down off your cross Malc!"

PHIL:

Earlier the evening had been pleasant and fun. We'd danced to the "Kerry Dancers" with Malcolm leading the song, and singing well too. Then as Hilda said, this fellow came in with a bottle, put on an act of the drunken seaman, and badgered Malcolm with, "Come on Malc, come on." They went back and forth putting their bottles upside down and drinking them empty. Malcolm became so drunk he needed help getting home. He fell when we were about halfway over and couldn't get up. Birney came along to help and there was Malcolm lying on the ground and Birney carrying on with, "Come down off your cross Malc."

While I was seeing him home Malcolm made some cryptic

statements that stayed with me for a long time. When he said something like "God knows," or "God will," there was always an extra tone, something apocalyptic to his utterances.

I remember that in one conversation he described the Spanish Civil War as a dark night that one would make it through. Then he talked about going out to the Far East on a ship. With his descriptions he took you into the situation: it was his job to bring the ashes up when they were cleaning out the furnaces, and throw them over the side. His ship was going past the Island of Sokotra and he said, "You couldn't get past Sokotra," and he kept repeating this. From what he said you could picture the oppressive heat and him coming up on deck to find that the island was still there, as if they had made no progress, as if the ship was caught in its own time warp. I also vaguely remember him telling me that there was a ruler on Sokotra who controlled everybody, like a despot of some remote time. And just as the ship couldn't physically get past Sokotra, this state of society couldn't be got past either. And he went on and on repeating, "You couldn't get past Sokotra."

I never had a conversation with Malcolm when he was sober, but when he was drunk he didn't think or speak in an ordinary context. There were expanding vibes from anything he said. He spoke in an apocalyptic manner from which one was supposed to see a phantasmagoric of relationships.... Part of his charisma was that he projected this strong emotional sense of something bigger than the event that was happening; he created a dimension about himself and events. An example of this quality was related to us by Margerie. When they were in Paris Malcolm went to the Grand Guignol. It was a great experience for him to see this rather gross and simplified kind of action because he would make it into tremendously dynamic drama. He went to see it again and again.

HILDA:

When the Lowrys left Vancouver they left a lot of manuscript behind. The shack was going to be torn down and when the bulldozers came in Norman and Gloria Levi rescued a suitcase full of manuscripts that otherwise would have been lost. The shack had been ransacked and there were papers all over the floor: postcards and letters, early versions of the *Volcano*, and bits of poems. Norman filled an old tin trunk approximately three feet by two feet by nine inches. Then the Levis went to Israel so they left the suitcase full of manuscripts with us for safekeeping.

That trunk and the manuscripts sat under our dining room table for what must have been two years. We used to get them out from time to time, read through them and try to decipher the handwriting. Having the manuscript collection in the house kept Lowry in my consciousness for a long time, and I did my Master's thesis on *Under the Volcano*. When Birney was collecting Lowry's papers, the Levis were still away, so we gave the trunk to the U.B.C. library.

Hilda Thomas (b.1928) has been a lecturer and senior instructor at the University of B.C. since 1963. Her Master's thesis, completed in 1965, is entitled "Malcolm Lowry's *Under the Volcano*: an interpretation." Her review of the *Selected Letters of Malcolm Lowry* was published in *Canadian Literature* 29 (Summer, 1966): pp. 56 – 58; her article "Lowry's Letters" was published in *Malcolm Lowry: The Man And His Work*, edited by George Woodcock (1971), pp. 103 – 109.

Phil Thomas (b. 1921) taught in the B.C. public school system from 1952 until his retirement. He is also a child art specialist and a folk song collector; he has published a collection of western Canadian folk songs entitled *Songs of the Pacific Northwest*. According to Phil, the "P.J. Thomas Collection" at the B.C. Provincial Archives (Sound and Moving Images Division) has three recordings of Margerie Lowry: in item 317 Margerie is singing Lowry's ballad "On a May Morning"; in item 318 Margerie is singing a fragment of "The Faithful Sailor-Boy," which she claims Lowry learned from one of the Dollarton fishermen; in item 319 Margerie comments that "On a May Morning" was written by Lowry to fool his professors into thinking they had discovered an original old English ballad, and that this occurred.

"He Made Art Out of Life"

George Robertson first met Lowry in 1949 at Earle Birney's Dollarton party. An aspiring writer, he was a student in Birney's Creative Writing class and was a member of *Authors Anonymous*. Although Robertson did not come to know Lowry intimately, he was captivated by the man and his writings. In 1961 he produced a two-part television documentary on Lowry for the C.B.C., the

75

result of an "awareness of Lowry's presence. . . even though he was gone." From an interview conducted in May 1985 Robertson recalls the following memorable encounters:

Like many of the other young people who met Malcolm at Earle's party, I was excited by the fact that he was there. I had read *Under the Volcano* and knew that Malcolm was an artist; he used language in a way that excited me. I think we all felt that *Volcano* was a book of major importance and that this man who had chosen to live out at Dollarton was a "great writer." We had heard from Earle that he was shy, reclusive, and had a drinking problem, which added to the fascination.

Malcolm had fortified himself with alcohol in order to meet strangers. When he arrived he took a position against a wall and people then approached him. I was extremely impressed by his voice, which was not deep, but low, quiet and well-spoken, intense; by his stocky frame and barrel-chest; by his exceedingly gentle manner; and most particularly by his eyes, which glittered with a demonic intensity. He recited from memory his poem "Sestina in a Cantina" [Appendix 3]. Perhaps I had never heard a sestina before (a verse form that depends upon the constant reiteration of a few words as the last words of each line) but I was hypnotized by him and by the poem.

I later ran into Malcolm and Margerie in downtown Vancouver and recall that we jogged along Pender Street whistling "I Can't Get Started With You." Malcolm recognized me from Earle's party and I was immediately and generously taken into his world of friends that he could talk to about writing. It didn't matter that I was a recent graduate with a few scribbles, it was the fact that I wanted to be a writer that made him accept my presence and open up.

I also encountered Malcolm one Sunday morning in the early summer of 1950. I was walking through the Hotel Vancouver lobby with Daryl Duke, also a recent graduate [now a Canadian television and film producer], when we met our former Modern English professor, Hunter Lewis. Dylan Thomas had given a reading in Vancouver the night before and Hunter said, "I need your help. I'm going upstairs to take Dylan Thomas out for breakfast and then to the airport. He's been up all night drinking with the Lowrys and God knows what condition they'll be in."

We entered Thomas' room expecting, since it was about ten in the morning, to find these people who'd been drinking all night laid out on the floor. Instead we found a most calm and sober group of people: Dylan Thomas was sitting on the bed cross-legged; Malcolm and Margerie were sitting on the floor with their backs to a wall; they were all still drinking and the conversation was very intelligent and quiet. Malcolm was describing a hallucination he had in a hospital while taking treatment for the d.t.'s. He said he was walking down a hall and arms and legs *burgeoned* (a wonderful use of the word) from the walls like plants or growths—a very striking image.

There wasn't any difficulty getting Thomas out of the room. He simply had to be reminded that it was time to go. As far as I can recall there was no concession made to Malcolm and Margerie as to what their plans were. It was just assumed that they would be ready to go home when we broke the party up.

Some time in the early part of 1954 I again ran into Malcolm and Margerie in downtown Vancouver, on West Pender Street. It was around five o'clock in the afternoon and they were in very good spirits. He'd had something to drink but he wasn't in any way out of control. They had been to Dale's Roast Chicken, a take-out place like Colonel

Panorama of the west side of the 500 block Granville Street showing Dale's Roast Chicken. (Circa 1940. Vancouver Public Library #5045.)

Sanders, and had purchased their evening meal. They were on their way to have a beer at the Niagara Hotel on Pender Street [Map 1] before catching the bus and said, "Come and have a beer. What are you doing? Why don't you come out to Dollarton with us and have some of this good roast chicken?" We went for a beer, only one, and chatted. Then we caught the bus to Dollarton at the terminal on Dunsmuir Street.

At dinner Malcolm poured us all gin to drink and the atmosphere was one of frolic and high spirits, added to by the pleasure of music and singing. After dinner I asked Malcolm to read some of his writings, which he did, but he was much more interested in reading T.E. Lawrence. I was feeling very pleased to be listening to Malcolm reading, but I drank very little in those days, and found the gin getting to my head fairly quickly. I fell asleep on a little couch in the living room. About six in the morning I woke up to the cries of the cormorants out in Burrard Inlet. I thought, "Oh my God, I've never done this before. How perfectly rude to fall asleep drunk in somebody's house, particularly when they are reading to you." Then after a little while I heard from their bedroom, which was separated from the living room only by a curtain that hung in the doorway, what to me was an unusual sound: Malcolm's voice stone cold sober saying to Margerie, "I wonder if George is awake?"

Malcolm came out from the bedroom and I said, "I'm awake and feel really embarrassed." He responded, "Why? Not at all." He cooked us breakfast and we talked; they were very sweet to me. It was a work day so I left after breakfast. Malcolm walked with me up the path and waited until the bus arrived

A letter Robertson wrote to the Lowrys highlights his overnight visit:

I remember my visit with you fondly, and I hope you are both well. It seems so long ago now. Do you remember you read me that poem whose title I have forgotten...of the sailor's last goodbye, and then you sang it to me, both of you, and played the guitar.[21] I can still remember most of the tune, and I still think it is one of the most beautiful things I have ever heard: I can still hear some of the cadences, and remember some of the words.... "as all who put their trust in the sea..." "...the green hills and blue mountains..." — I hope I'm not misquoting too much. I vowed I would put that music down on paper sometime, or get it put down for me, and I will yet. Perhaps someday you two will sing it into a tape recorder, and then somebody with musical savvy will transcribe it into notes....[22] My best wishes to both of you for fruitful and happy times (U.B.C. 1:59).

Robertson:

I had only one other communication from Malcolm and that was just before they went away in August 1954.

He phoned me a week or so before they were to leave and kindly said, "We're going to be in England for a while. The cabin is there if you wish to use it for a weekend or if you want to hole up there and do some writing. I've left it in charge of Harvey Burt, and I've told him about you so feel free to call him up." I never did stay in their cabin, and wasn't on the beach again until after Malcolm's death, when I filmed the shacks being bulldozed and burned.

Malcolm was obviously an interior sort of person. I think he had the drunkard's awareness that inanimate objects and people can sometimes conspire to assume proportions of evil or threat. But when he was among friends and people he trusted, and quite evidently among young people and would-be writers, he felt comfortable. He was touched by young people who wanted to write.

I never saw Malcolm, for all his problems, as pitiful. I suppose if I'd seen him weeping and desperate and falling down drunk, as I dare say he sometimes was, then I might have found that moment pitiful. But I don't think the essential person was. He was an artist. He made art out of life and that was the purpose of his life and his daemon. I respected his commitment and drive to create, but I did feel Malcolm was paying for it. That may be a very sentimental view but when you're young you do have very sentimental views.

He was an extraordinarily complex person and one that defies summing up easily; probably a good thing too. He was simply who he was.

———————

After graduating from U.B.C. in 1950, George Robertson (b. 1929) attended the Writers Workshop at the State University of Iowa; worked at the National Film Board from 1950 – 1953; and for the Canadian Broadcasting Corporation as a producer in radio (1953 – 1957) and television (1960 – 1968, 1969 to the present). He is currently a producer for *the fifth estate*.

———————

"A State of Emotional Turmoil"

Gloria Onley met Lowry through her first husband, Norman Newton, whom she had married in 1951 in Winnipeg, Manitoba. In 1952 Norman and Gloria moved to Vancouver, and Norman, who had known Lowry since 1949, renewed the acquaintanceship. The following is taken from an interview with Gloria Onley in January 1985:

> In the spring of 1953, Norman and I were living in a coach house in Shaughnessy. One Friday evening Norman received a phone call from Malcolm who was at a hotel in the Skid Road area.[23] He said he'd been there for some time and he'd been drinking. He sounded distressed, Norman thought, so we decided to go and find him.
>
> We had great difficulty finding the hotel from Malcolm's description, but eventually did and discovered Malcolm in a small room opening onto an air shaft. Malcolm told us that noises would come in from the air shaft during the night: sounds of beatings, of faceless people arguing, fighting and crying. Malcolm found this very disturbing; he seemed to feel that he was condemned to be in the room and could not of his own volition leave it. We gradually discovered that Margerie had gone to California for medical treatment and that, after her departure, Malcolm had started to drink, eventually abandoning their apartment for this hotel room where he had remained for some time in a state of helplessness. I got the impression that he was totally reliant on Margerie to keep him going and simply could not cope when she went away.
>
> Malcolm was in a state of emotional turmoil: he was worried about Margerie's health, yet he was upset because she had gone away to be treated, leaving him alone. He knew she had to go, to save her life, but he felt betrayed when she went.[24] Agonized by these incoherent feelings, he kept on drinking.
>
> When we got back to the coach house, after a terribly embarrassing taxi ride, Malcolm settled down on our living room couch and was there for the rest of the weekend, with occasional forays into the rest of the small living quarters. He would be sick intermittently, and insisted on continuing to drink, although we were trying to get him to stop. I was concerned because I realized he had stopped eating some time ago. I tried to get some food into him, at least some liquid nourishment. I remember heating up beef broth and making eggnogs. Malcolm would take a few spoonfuls to humour me, but most of it would come back up a short time later.
>
> We didn't really know what to do. Malcolm seemed to be, at least part of the time, in an advanced stage of alcoholism. He would drowse off and then wake up shouting or crying, returning to consciousness

through what must have been a short period of *delirium tremens*. He had a nose bleed at one point, causing us further anxiety. If it had not stopped, or if his general condition had become any worse, we would have called for an ambulance or a doctor. Malcolm kept saying he would be all right and did not want to see a doctor.

When I saw Malcolm he wasn't at his most lovable. He was vomiting at intervals and only marginally able to look after himself. He certainly wasn't able to shave or wash up by himself. He would throw up and then I'd get a towel and washcloth and help him to clean himself up.

We didn't have a bathroom in the coach house, just a cold water tap. It was technically substandard living accommodation, although it had been made into a very pleasant, contemporary living space by its former tenant, a designer. There was a bathroom in the basement of the house across the driveway—the house to which the coach house belonged. We shared this bathroom with the tenants of the basement suite. Norman had to take Malcolm across to use the toilet every so often, and these people saw Malcolm once or twice. They were angry at us for bringing someone who was obviously a drunk into their bathroom. It was a very embarrassing and difficult situation; we could

The Shaughnessy area coach house where Lowry spent a few days "recovering" in the spring of 1953. The building has changed little since then. (Photo taken in 1986.)

not explain ourselves adequately, and were even afraid of being evicted. The coach house was not a good place for Malcolm to be, although it seemed to bother us far more than it did him.

Malcolm seemed to be trying to move out of his blurred state, to attend to his duty as a guest by conversing with us. But much of the time his speech consisted of literary statements, rhetorical questions and aphorisms, as if he were attempting to enlighten and perhaps even to entertain us, but not actually to have a dialogue with us. He would talk partly to himself and partly to us, or to whichever one of us happened to be there, and it was often as if a writer were musing aloud. He might have been quoting himself, repeating something he had written or said on some previous occasion. There were many aphorisms about life and the agonies of various dilemmas. I remembered many of them for a long time and even wrote some of them down afterward, but with the passage of years, eventually I lost my notes and forgot what he had said, remembering only that he did make some truly significant statements.

Otherwise he talked about being in the hotel, being alone, and at least implied that he realized he had a problem with his drinking. I think he also talked about Margerie and living with her in Vancouver, about his childhood and his father, about writing and publishing. I gathered from things he said that he would often almost involuntarily do really idiotic things, such as getting into a roaring fight with the landlord over a trivial matter and being evicted because of it. His egocentricity and paranoia must have made life extremely difficult for Margerie and for other people too, as they would become drawn into Malcolm's personal dramas.

The time that Malcolm spent with us that weekend was exhausting and frustrating but intensely interesting. His presence filled me with anxiety and melancholy; I remember thinking, "Oh God! Here's someone in a truly pitiful state. What can I do to help him?" We couldn't seem to do anything that would really help him; we were just keeping him from getting any worse. We were somehow committed to keeping him alive, although it almost seemed an act of cruelty to inflict eggnogs and washcloths on him. I think the most important thing we did for him was just to keep him company; when he did not have a firm grip on reality, he obviously found being alone terrifying and devastating. To keep from going mad, he needed at least one other person to be with him. I felt we were filling up the void until Margerie came back, in this way enabling him to survive. But we were mired down ourselves. We couldn't leave or give up; it was like being on a treadmill.

It was difficult to feel any real rapport with Malcolm because he was in a completely different state of consciousness. It would have been insensitive and irresponsible to drink with him, and would not have brought us any closer to him. Under the circumstances, I would have been frightened to abandon my objectivity.

I had read *Under the Volcano* and I was very much in awe of the man and his genius. At the same time, I felt exasperated with him because he couldn't cope with life. I wanted to help him, but at the same time I wondered whether he was not, in some sense, being self-indulgent. I also recall feeling acute twinges of exasperation because part of the time he was definitely in a histrionic mood, giving a performance on our small stage. At times he seemed to be actually enjoying his ability to utter aphorisms about his inner agony, as if he were a playwright creating himself as a character in his own play. There were flashes of exultation and power, as if, far from being out of control, he could in fact find no better or higher use for himself than to be burnt out and consumed by the process of his art.

Malcolm was pleasant to me during those moments when he seemed most in touch with mundane reality. He seemed to be aware that I had never seen anyone in his state before, that I had no precedent for my dealings with him. He was so mired down in his condition, I wished for an antidote to magically cure him. The next morning, with naive good will I picked a flower from the garden around the coach house and brought it to him. It might have been a narcissus, it might have been a daffodil; it was a fresh, beautiful spring flower. He took it with a wry smile and said something half-chagrined, half-charming. I felt terribly young, and very unsuccessful in my symbolism.

Norman eventually found someone who could come and take Malcolm over to Bowen Island to Einar and Muriel Neilson's. I felt tremendously relieved that I wouldn't have to deal with such a difficult situation any longer, and that Malcolm was going where experienced people could look after him. Malcolm stayed with the Neilsons for several days, possibly until Margerie returned. Muriel knew how to look after him: she was an older woman who was an elementary school teacher on the Island. She was used to dealing with naughty children, and I think she probably dealt with Malcolm in a similar way, at least to some extent. Because I was so young, it was impossible for me to be any kind of authority figure to a man in his early forties.

This experience with Malcolm later caused me to speculate about the relationship between drinking and creativity, to wonder whether alcohol had a liberating effect on one's literary imagination. I wanted to be a writer and I remember wondering whether getting a bit drunk would improve my ability to write. I did try it on one occasion, and it didn't work at all; after that, I abandoned the idea.

Seven years after this extraordinary weekend, I was to draw on the experience to begin a television drama about an encounter between a world-weary alcoholic man and a naive girl. I never finished the play, for I could never arrive at any meaningful resolution of this encounter of opposites. My relationship with Malcolm, if you could call it that, was similarly never developed, and my feelings about the artistic creativity he exemplified were to remain forever ambivalent.

At the time Gloria Onley (b. 1930) met Malcolm Lowry, she had graduated the previous year from the University of Manitoba with a B.A. in English and Philosophy; in 1966 she obtained a Master's Degree in English from the University of B.C. Her published writing consists mainly of literary criticism; during the early 1970s she became, for a few years, a major critic of Margaret Atwood. Her marriage to artist Toni Onley in 1961 involved her in visual arts management; in 1976 she became an art publisher, and since 1981 she has had a print gallery on Granville Island in Vancouver.

"Balancing on the Rim of the Abyss"

Norman Newton first met Lowry in 1949, and Lowry considered him to be "an exceptionally promising writer" (*Selected Letters*, 410). Newton was encouraged by Lowry and viewed him as a "master." In January 1986 Newton wrote the following recollections in a letter to the author, adding to those of Gloria Onley and including other impressions and memories. When Lowry stayed at the coach house Newton recalls:

> I [...got] a bottle from the liquor store. As Gloria says, Malcolm could not keep any food down and I understood he had not eaten for a long time. There was no question of cutting off his liquor and letting him "sweat it out." I had never encountered *delirium tremens* but his state resembled what I had read of it. I was afraid that if we simply cut off his liquor supply we would bring on a serious mental, perhaps also physical, crisis. Only a doctor could have made a decision such as this.
>
> I reasoned that the only way we could get some nourishment into him was to mix gin with tomato juice, give him drinks when he demanded them, and gradually reduce the gin until there was nothing in the glass but tomato juice. I had to go to work the morning after we picked him up,[25] and I believe I told Gloria to give him these mock drinks at fairly regular intervals, at the same time trying to contact Margerie. He was not to be told we were "treating" him in this way (that is, with the old Skid Road treatment of "tapering off"). He and we knew that the amount of gin in the glass was gradually being reduced, but the illusion that he was "having drinks" was to be kept up. I think that this was the first time that I realised there was something infantile about his drinking. He knew, of course, that there was little or no gin in the glass but the illusion that he was "having a drink" would be carefully maintained. He would consent to take some food if he could play the game of "having a drink." It impressed me as

rather like thumb-sucking, a nipple substitute. We were "playing doctor" and he was "being patient," in spite of the fact that the situation was perfectly and for us frighteningly real. . . .

When I came home [from work] Malcolm had a better colour. He was lying on the couch pretending to be asleep. I think this gave me more insight into him than anything he ever did while he was awake, drunk or sober. The insight shocked me. It must be remembered that I had simply been overwhelmed by *Under the Volcano*, and that I thought of Lowry as a superior being, a *poète maudit* in the grand romantic tradition, trailing sulphurous clouds of glory. I was in a state of naive hero-worship, as you can see. But Lowry on the couch had the careful rigidity of limb, the slight half-smile which seems about to break into a giggle, the somewhat squinty tension about the closed eyes which characterises a seven-year-old who has done something rather naughty or has been caught after "lights out" and is pretending to be fast asleep.

The strange and rather horrible thing, however, is that he resembled a perfectly normal and healthy seven-year-old. It was a real regression, even to the muscles. . . . I had thought of him as a kind of drunken god — his favourite role in my presence — but now I began to see that there was something terribly incomplete about him. I definitely do *not* mean sexually incapable, since I had a naive vision of he and Margerie as Venus and Mars on some kind of alcoholic Olympus. I do not even mean that he was infantile in the sense that he liked to be mothered: everybody wants to be fussed over from time to time. I mean that it struck me, engendering a feeling of horror, that there was some kind of dreadful "hole" in his mind, that in a sense he had never lived at all, or, worse, that his experiences as an adult had somehow consumed each other and that he was "empty," "eaten out," had simply lost his adult personality.

These are pretty heavy deductions to make from a glimpse of a man pretending to be asleep. But that was what I felt, though the intensity of the feeling was muffled by the practical necessities of the situation. At that point my attitude towards him and the kind of poetic vision he so splendidly embodied changed absolutely. I continued to admire his genius and to love him as a man, but the hero-worship had gone.

There was the immediate practical problem of what to do with him. I could not quit my job to take care of him. . . [and Gloria] could not take care of him any longer. He needed professional help, at least somebody who knew him well enough to help him out of his state of collapse. (Later according to Day [who wrote *Malcolm Lowry: A Biography*], it was discovered that he had been walking around for some days with a couple of broken ribs; but, as Gloria says, he kept insisting there was nothing wrong with him).

We had been phoning around to some friends who also knew Lowry and one of them. . . reminded us of the Neilsons [on Bowen

Lowry at "Lieben" on Bowen Island. (Birney Papers, University of Toronto.)

Island]....Muriel was a marvellously practical and motherly woman; Einar was a man's man who had knocked about the world long enough to know how to cope with advanced alcoholism....We had been able to get through to Margerie in Los Angeles (Malcolm had given us the number) and she came back to Vancouver as soon as she could....

I remember a silly game we played with the radio the night before Lowry left for Bowen Island.[26] One radio station was solemnly describing the funeral of some dignitary, and another was broadcasting, if I remember correctly, descriptions of lost dogs and other pets. By random switching between these stations, we constructed some kind of aleatory farce which had him roaring with laughter and sent him off to sleep feeling relaxed.

I remember trying to shave him the next day. He enjoyed my tucking the towel around his neck and lathering his face, quite like a nice little boy having his hair combed. I had never shaved anybody but myself and the job was a messy one but at least I did not cut him. I was struck again by the childlike way he enjoyed things being done for him. . . .

We [first] met at a party of Earle Birney's writing students, held in Birney's shack in Dollarton, two away from Lowry's own. . . . [27] For my part I was most impressed by something strange, almost uncanny about the way he held himself. His body was barrel-shaped and stiff; his arms were short and his hands small; his legs were thick. He wore a sort of embarrassed grin, something between a comically wolfish leer and the embarrassed "silly ass" grin of caricatured Englishmen in the movies. He moved in a rocking motion which might indeed remind one of the seaman's rolling gait but also resembled the movements of a robot. Yet his eyes had a feline glitter and they were extraordinarily alive, not the aliveness of the quick-witted observer but more like that (I know how inappropriate this sounds but I simply retail my impressions) of a predator or sorcerer. I had never met a man who embodied in such a physically apparent manner the soul-body duality: he seemed to live in his body as if it were a tank.

At a distance. . . his face, with its moustache, handsome beakish nose, wide mouth and strong chin, his high broad forehead, his muscular stocky body. . . suggested a strong and sensual man, capable of command. . . . But a closer view. . . suggested that this deteriorating but virile and rather coarsely handsome body imprisoned an Ariel-like spirit, all light and fire, who not only did not know what to do with it but actively resented it. . . .

He had the most Protean character of any man I have ever known; . . . this character was completely embedded in his literary vision; . . . I was too much in awe of him to separate my admiration of his writing from my sense of him as a person. But like everybody else I was struck by his elaborate gestures of modesty and courtesy, by his freedom from petty, self-serving acts, and by his complete and almost suicidal indifference to the practical concerns of everyday life. One thing which must be remembered is that, until the events. . . [at the coach house] I was more of a disciple than a friend. . . . As I was more than willing to follow him into his vision at the time, it was more the case of a naive young man having great fellow-feeling for somebody he considers a master. . . .

He was a very dramatic person in my presence, always performing. He had something of the style of the old Shakesperian actor, and at times seemed to belong in the company of Dylan Thomas (as a performer) and Sir Donald Wolfit. . . . When he and Margerie were entertaining me in their shack at Dollarton, the mood was one of high intellectual delight interspersed with moments of Falstaffian (though not indecent) humour and sheer incoherence — but I remember few details because we were all drunk. . . . I [do] recall one of Malcolm's songs, sung to the tune of "Daddy wouldn't buy me a bow-wow" —

Daddy wouldn't buy me a Mau-Mau!
Daddy wouldn't buy me a Mau-mau!
He bought a strangled cat,
And I'm very fond of that,
BUT—
Daddy wouldn't buy me a Mau-mau!

This came in the middle of a story about voodoo. His singing was quite unmusical, and he accompanied himself with a furious and rattly strumming on the ukulele which would have caused embarrassment at a YMCA picnic.

Malcolm had an intensely musical mind—his writing uses rhetorical devices in the style of an accomplished composer—but he had none of the physical endowments of the musician. His sense of pitch was poor; his physical coordination was not refined enough to enable him to master an instrument; his musculature and joints seemed made for heavy labour and prevented the delicacy and finesse of gesture which the performing musician needs. He was also, Day implies, sexually clumsy. All this, of course, went to feed his hatred of his body. It simply did not respond finely enough. I feel that his lack of physical finesse had something to do with his failure to master the craft of verse. The images are marvellous, but the ear is coarse so far as rhythmic detail is concerned. He needed the larger and looser swing of prose.

He was not aware of much outside himself. Most of his favourite reading was of authors who had made their reputations in the 1920s and 1930s. He had no small talk and few opinions; he did not engage in "polite conversation." He opened his mouth and images rushed out, inchoate fragments of literature for the most part. When he stopped, I would do the same. A very strange form of communication, now I think of it. If one of us had stopped talking for a moment, the silence would have been oppressive and painful. . . . There could be no true interaction between him and me; I was too young.

He was certainly pursued by demons in the same way as the Consul; but he would always turn this pursuit into crazy humour when he was talking with me; he was leading the demons a "merry chase," balancing on the rim of the abyss. I must say that knowing Lowry confirmed me as a Christian and a Swedenborgian Christian at that. He convinced me of the reality of hell. I do not think of him as quite the "Faustian" figure of *Under the Volcano.* . . . No, Lowry thought he could play games with hell. He was doing a tightrope dance over the abyss in sheer childish bravado; he was a drunken sailor out of a ballad by Didbin. Yes, he fell in and was horribly tortured by demons I believe to be real. Of course, I am not saying he was "damned." Rather, he was torn apart. His motive was a desperate poetic bravado, not the desire to do evil. Nobody could have been *less* evil than the Lowry I knew. His great talent aside, he was a foolish, reckless boy excited by his own fear. . . . He was so deep in his private world that he seemed to present no exterior self which could be wounded. He would emerge from this world crying and wanting help—as in the Skid Road incident—and then he seemed like a child wanting to be parented, dependent rather than "vulnerable." There was nothing of easily-wounded vanity or *amour-propre* continually demanding to be soothed. . . .

Feelings of inferiority? Not in the conventional sense. He had no social role, no job; he had abandoned his parental family and rejected his background. There is some talk about inferiority feelings in Day; but perhaps Lowry was simply obliging the psychiatrists by dragging up what he thought would interest them. He was, by choice, completely outside social life. Eventually it terrified him. He was overwhelmed by it like a neolithic villager suddenly thrust into the middle of New York traffic. Feelings of "inferiority" hardly describe the panic that seizes one in such a situation. . . . He was plagued by a monstrous assemblage of guilts and self-doubtings, but the inner turmoil was such that any external slight was hardly noticed. . . . I would describe him as "self-lacerating" rather than vulnerable. . . . He was not sensitive to the needs of others because he could not get outside himself. He *tried* to be sensitive. He made the most extravagant gestures of politeness and consideration, but they were always a little bit "off" because he was either too drunk or self-absorbed to read the situation. I did not see the bad side Day writes about. I saw a man trying so painfully hard to be good and kind that the memory of it almost brings tears to my eyes; but there was something comic about it too, because he was always mistiming the gesture and poking you in the eye when he meant to embrace you. . . .

I don't think Malcolm was ever comfortable. He was extremely ebullient or very depressed. I never saw him in an ordinary or average state. For the same reason I cannot say what made him uncomfortable. These words are meaningless for a person so influenced by his own swings of mood. The description of him as a mild manic-depressive, which I find in Day, rings true in the pop-psychology sense; but the problem is that a part of him always remained very rational indeed, as if he were riding his own wild moods like a roller-coaster. I did not have the impression of anything like insanity, even in a mild form. I had the impression of somebody "playing with his mind," a habit which had become compulsive. (There are some men who feel they are dead and decaying creatures unless they are in a state of near-tumescence all the time; perhaps there is a psychic equivalent of this). I think Malcolm was afraid of being "comfortable." He had internalised, with desperate literalness and with hair-raising success, the romantic image of the *poète maudit*.

William Empson's comment, "I think his life was ruined by a mistaken critical theory. . ." (Kilgallin, 19) sounds dry and professorial, yet I think it is closer to the truth than anything I have read. Certainly much closer than the speculations of Day. It must not be forgotten that the world of the poetic imagination is a real one, not a pleasant dream. It has its brothels and thieves' kitchens; it has its deserts, seas and forests where one may be lost or shipwrecked. If one chooses to haunt only its wild and dangerous places as a "thrill-seeker," a certain appearance of mental imbalance may be induced and something like insanity may finally result. But I do not think the psychiatrists know much about this world.

Malcolm was extremely kind about my writing. He praised it, but more for the potential it showed than for its value as finished work. I walked on air for days, as you might expect. . . . I knew that my work was a mixture of the good and the merely raw. The great value of Lowry's praise to me was that he singled out the parts I instinctively felt were most successful. This gave me more faith in my own judgement. . . . But I should add that Margerie made some very acute and occasionally harsh comments. Her ideas on literature were not really as deep as Malcolm's but showed considerable concision and practicality. By the way, some writer on Lowry should give Margerie the credit she deserves, to counterbalance the feline snideness of Day's portrayal, which is doubly unjust because Day owed so much to her. I noticed many of his [Malcolm's] acquaintances and friends falling into the trap of seeming vulnerability which he so cleverly set [and that they] began to feel a quasi-erotic protectiveness, which led to a peculiar *jealousy* of Margerie. I seem to recognize this quality in Day. I am convinced that without Margerie we would have no *Under the Volcano*; I doubt that Lowry would have lived long enough to write the book and I am certain he would never have been able to finish it. Lowry was a great writer, but she was an admirable and strong person. I do not recognize her in the "starlet" cliches of Day's biography. They were both "performers," of course, a theatrical couple; but Day does not know the difference between theatricality and self-deception.

We did not talk about other writers. I was too greedy for help with my own work. The only Canadian writer I heard him praise was Birney, for his novel *Turvey*.[28] But his letters show that he was very generous in his praise for others. . . . Malcolm profoundly influenced me in the religious sense, because his agony was so obviously spiritual. He did not much influence me as a writer. At the height of my hero-worship I found myself writing a few pages which were frankly imitative, but they were bombastic pastiche. When I was able to take a more balanced view of his work I was able to appreciate it for the first time. . . . [For] his influence on my "life" — all I can do is quote the well-known lines of Hopkins —

O the mind, mind has mountains; cliffs of fall
Frightful, sheer, no-man-fathomed. Hold them cheap
May who ne'er hung there...

Malcolm entered this landscape rashly, without preparation. You will have heard about Central Asian shamans who travel into spiritual realms, "riding" on their drums. Malcolm's drum was alcohol, and the only intellectual guide he had was a rough assemblage of magical ideas. He paid terribly for this rashness. But the most marvellous thing was that he found, in his degradation, an immense compassion for other men. Without this "cosmic pity," *Under the Volcano* would only be a remarkable work of drunken rhetoric. Locked in the closet of his alcohol-soaked body, crying out in fear and horror, he found that he was crying out *for others*. This is what gives the book its tragic beauty. I really do believe that Malcolm had himself to blame for his predicament but he found a spring of generous feeling in his degradation which enabled him to speak for the truly victimised and exploited.

The effect on my "life" was similar to that of witnessing and to some extent participating in a tragic event which offers a brief but powerful perception of spiritual realities which are normally hidden to us. It is tragic because it involves tragic pride, a desperate storming of precipices which are meant to be climbed one foothold at a time. I think of Malcolm as dying in some remote and terrible wilderness which most of us know nothing of, a place he himself had chosen. But when I think that he was enabled to find a universal meaning, even a tortured beauty, in this fate I think of what I shall call, without theological presumptions in this case, "redemptive mercy."

In his youth Norman Newton (b. 1929) supported himself by acting and writing for theatre and the C.B.C. He has studied musical composition with Jean Coulthard and Tiber Serly, and has composed music for radio plays, film, and chamber works for groups. Newton is the author of six books of prose and verse; has published verse and critical articles; wrote the award-winning one-act play *The Rehearsal*, and the libretto for the prize winning opera *Seabird Island*; and has won many awards, including the Canada Music Council Award for the best orchestral reading of Canadian music. Newton works for the C.B.C. and lives in Vancouver with his wife and daughter.

" 'There's Always Hope if You Can Hang on to It' "

Noel Stone drove Lowry from the Newtons' home in Vancouver to the ferry terminal at Horseshoe Bay. He escorted Lowry on the ferry to Bowen Island, where they both visited with Einar and Muriel Neilson. Stone passed the days alone, swimming, reading, and relaxing; he passed the evenings with Lowry and the Neilsons, enjoying dinner and conversation. The following recollections were recorded in September 1985:

> Norman Newton came along with us on the drive to the ferry terminal. He was very good about looking after Malcolm, very solicitous. In fact, I think I upset Norman a little because of the response I had to a generous comment he made about Malcolm in his presence: he said Malcolm was the greatest writer of the twentieth century. I thought that would be embarrassing to Malcolm, and I said, "Oh take it easy Norman," at which he looked disgruntled. However, Malcolm looked as though he loved Norman's comment, so I was probably off base in reacting as I did.
>
> Malcolm was recovering from a binge and other adventures I don't know about. He was quiet and rather withdrawn but I noticed that he had a sheepish little smile and a way of looking at you in which he was obviously sizing you up. Like a child, he was very quick in deciding who was going to be friendly towards him; I think he was sizing me up to see what kind of friend I was going to be.
>
> Once we were on the ferry, we were alone for the duration of the twenty minute ride. This then gave me an opportunity to talk privately with him. I had read *Volcano* for the first time shortly before, and I started to talk about the book because I wanted him to know how much it had impressed me. Malcolm then told me something I've never forgotten. He said, "But, you know I was wrong. I was wrong in the book." And I said, "In what way?" He replied, "The book leaves the reader with no hope. There's always hope if you can hang on to it."
>
> Shortly after we arrived at the Neilsons', Einar started to show us improvements he'd been making to the property. Muriel caught my sleeve, pulled me aside, and said, "Have you brought anything to drink?" When I replied that I had a bottle of rum she said, "Where is it? Give it to me." Muriel was wise in the way of alcoholics and she knew that any liquor had to be kept out of Malcolm's reach. So I gave her the bottle.
>
> Malcolm interacted with the Neilsons in a very comfortable way. They were warm people who knew how to draw him out, and he responded. Over dinner they made conversation about other visitors they'd had and the work they were doing on their house. They had a variety of theories that they wanted to discuss. For example, Einar

talked about his ideas on domestic architecture. He had built their house without interior walls, his idea being that nothing should be hidden, everything should be open, even when the house was full of visitors. Malcolm listened respectfully and made some comments, but for the most part he sat quietly.

We had a pleasant dinner and evening with the Neilsons and afterwards were escorted to their guest house. I took out my toiletries, shoved my overnight bag under my bunk, and went to sleep. I have never told about an incident that took place during the night because I thought it would reflect unkindly. Now I can see that's not really so. During the night I heard a rustling noise and woke up thinking there were mice on the floor. Moonlight was shining through the window and when I looked down Malcolm was going through my bag. I said, "What's going on Malcolm?" He looked up at me without a trace of embarrassment and said, "Good God man, haven't you brought anything to drink?" I said, "No, there's nothing there." He said, "Got

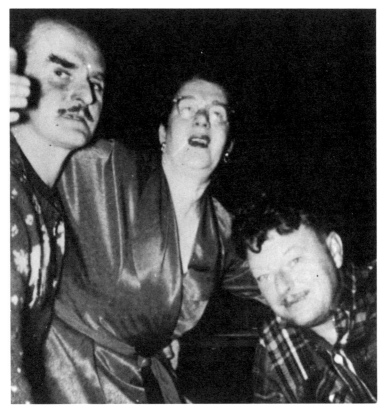

Lowry with Einar and Muriel Neilson at their home on Bowen Island. (Birney Papers, University of Toronto.)

to have it old man. Got to have it." So I said, "Well you won't find any there," and took my bag and pushed it back underneath the bed. He got up and paced around, and we talked for a while. I eventually got back to sleep but he had quite a restless night, nothing dramatic, no d.t.'s.[29] The next night he seemed to sleep more easily, and by the end of the weekend he appeared to be feeling better.

I received a nice note from him a week later, thanking me for taking him to the Neilsons'. I'm sorry I didn't keep it as a memento.

Noel Stone (b. 1927) graduated with a B.A. from the University of B.C. in 1951. In the early 1950s he worked as an announcer and producer for the C.B.C.; from 1954 – 1957 he was a film scriptwriter, and a television director in England; from 1958 – 1963 he worked for the National Film Board of Canada (Montreal) as a writer and director. At this point he disappeared into the backwoods of B.C. and little has been heard of him since.

"Up in a Tree Drunk"

Ben Maartman purchased a shack on the Dollarton beach in the early 1950s. He gave Norman and Gloria Levi use of the shack, and did not move in himself until after the Lowrys had left the beach in 1954. Through his membership in *Authors Anonymous* and his visits with the Levis, Maartman had some memorable interactions with Lowry:

> The first time I met Malcolm we were moving a stove down the bank to the Levis'. Malcolm was up in a tree, drunk and making strange noises. He said a cougar had come after him so he'd climbed the tree. He was stuck and we helped him out. In turn he insisted on helping us with the stove, which amounted to pushing all three of us and the stove straight down the cliff, knocking the stove's legs off!
>
> One afternoon I went out to visit the Levis and Malcolm was reading something about "horrors, horrors,"[30] and I said, "Well with all these horrors you must have been in a whorehouse." That I should make fun of Malcolm when he was reading was unforgivable. He said that I was the devil and he was God and we were about to have it out. He was outraged but I thought it was funny.
>
> I used to kid him just to get him going. I had been in the navy during the war, and had worked as a fisherman, so when Malcolm would talk

94

about *Ultramarine* I would call him a "bloody cookie": a cookie at sea is the guy who is the mess boy. And I'd say things like, "You couldn't tie up your shoelaces for Christ sake, what were you doing on a boat?" or "Wrung more sea water out of my socks then you've ever seen Malcolm"; this sort of banter just to turn Malcolm on. He would go into classics about seafaring, and he would point across the inlet to the tank farm with its flares and say, "That's hell over there and that's where you're going!"[31]

I didn't really have that much to do with the Lowrys because they were very reclusive and whatever I did it would always seem to make things worse. I was somewhat unpopular with Margerie because I drove Malcolm down to the Lynnwood [Map 2] a few times to get a box [of beer] but, of course, before we got the box we'd close the place. Margerie would be furious. She was the only person I have ever heard scream in iambic pentameter. She must have practiced it for hours while we were at the pub and then she would unload on Malcolm. To me it was funnier than hell. It was also part of life on the beach, where at night you would get strange combinations: the flares from the Shell refinery making it look like hell had burst loose; Margerie singing these beautiful bloody incantations of what was going to happen to Malcolm, and to me too, because she knew I was the transportation; voices, out of the night and mist, from the fishermens' radios as their boats went up and down the inlet; the old

A view of the Dollarton beach with Margerie in the doorway of the Lowrys' shack. (Courtesy of Margerie Lowry.)

"whoo whoo wa whoo" of the train as it went thundering along its main line on the other side of the inlet, and of course on foggy nights the Point Atkinson foghorn [Map 4].

When he'd get drunk Malcolm would speak with a flow of thoughts and imagery. He would look at something like the local gravel pit and tell you all the shades of history, and classics down through the times, and out of it would come a kernel of why we were all in this moment in time. His knowledge, associations, and descriptions were phenomenal. He was a poet: we could all have the same experience but he was the only one who could capture it.

When he was drunk he had flushed cheeks, which made a striking combination with his very bright eyes, mischievous smile, and very white, sharp teeth. Many of the Dollarton locals thought he was crazy and some saw him as a threat. I remember somebody down on the beach saying, "If that crazy son of a bitch comes around here he'll get it." Poor old Malcolm, he couldn't harm anybody.

The nice thing about the Lowrys' shack was that it jutted out on the foreshore and got the first light from the east and had light all day. In mine I was blind sided from the east so I didn't get as much sun or as much view as they did. They also had one or two shacks that they kept things in. After they left the beach I went down to one of these shacks; it may have been the one they called the "mink's house." There wasn't a door on it, and the shack was empty except for a clutter of manuscripts and letters. I presumed Malcolm had kept it all because it was of value to him, so I gathered it up. One of the letters was from Conrad Aiken and he described his new teeth as "things of dazzling beauty and tolerable speed."

I decided to keep the papers for him because Harvey Burt was living in Lowry's shack and I fully expected he and Margerie to return. I kept the papers in a box under the bed where my roommate slept. His bed sagged and he wanted the papers moved, but I said, "No, you're sleeping on genius, just get comfortable with it." The papers eventually went to the University of B.C.

Ben Maartman (b. 1924) worked as a commercial fisherman, and as a social worker and parole officer in the province of British Columbia. He also spent some time working as a freelance writer for the C.B.C. He is now retired and spends his time with his family, travelling, and writing. He is currently working on a novel.

"The Outside World Was the Adding Machine of Hell"

Gloria and Norman Levi lived on the Dollarton beach in the summer of 1954, two shacks southwest of the Lowrys'. Gloria sometimes went for walks along the beach with Lowry, and found him to be a sympathetic listener as well as a supersensitive individual. Her recollections are reprinted from Tony Kilgallin's book, *Lowry* (p. 69).

> My first impression was of him sitting sober in a corner of his shack like a little monastery boy, with his face averted, not even willing to say hello. He was so sensitive that he had to return a valuable painting he had received from a Paris artist because it was too painful to behold. To him the outside world was the adding machine of hell; when he read his works to us he imitated the sounds of the trees in the wind because here was Paradise. When he wrote he lived a very Spartan existence; he'd rise at five or six, eat very lightly, swim, work until ten or eleven, swim again then repeat this routine throughout the day going to bed early. He would do this for a period until he'd explode, and then it was just drinking and lolling around. Then the only thing that put the skin back on his nerves was gin and playing Elizabethan madrigals on his tiple when entertaining friends. His advice to my husband on writing was: "First know what you want to say, then sit on it for a long-long time, even a year at least before you even start writing, while you think it through. It's how long you live with the idea that shows you whether it's worthwhile to write it."

The Levis reside in Vancouver and Norman is a former New Democratic Party Member of the Legislative Assembly in B.C. He salvaged a large collection of manuscript, correspondence, and other papers from one of the Lowrys' storage shacks; these are now housed in the Special Collections Library at the University of B.C.

"The Joy of Living Beside the Lowrys"

Harvey Burt and his wife Dorothy were weekend and summer residents of the Dollarton beach. They met the Lowrys in the early 1950s, purchased a neighbouring shack, and became close friends.[32] When the Lowrys moved from the beach to England in 1954, they entrusted the Burts with the care of their shack, their boat *My Heart's in the Highlands,* as well as the large collection of books and papers they left behind. In a letter written to the Burts in the spring of 1956, Lowry indicates a deep emotional attachment to his Dollarton home. He wrote, "The more things of mine, ours—books, for example—that are left there the less desolated it will look, also *feel* from this end.... Childish though it may seem, there is the pier, which we built, which I cannot imagine myself living without, even if it isn't there or myself am dead" (*Selected Letters,* 386 – 387).

The following recollections are reprinted from Tony Kilgallin's book, *Lowry* (pp. 60 – 68).

We had the privilege and joy of living beside the Lowrys for two and a half years, though we were not permanent residents. We did, however, spend week-ends at the beach, and were down two or three times during the week besides. When we first arrived in the spring of 'fifty-two, we were warned by Margerie not to disturb Malcolm during the day because he was working, but it was not long before Margerie or Malcolm would shout across to us as soon as they knew we had arrived. From then on we saw them and visited with them at least twice a week, sometimes for a whole day at a time.

While we knew them, they had very few visitors: Margerie valiantly encouraged Malcolm to write, and Malcolm had an instinctive or acquired distrust of people who "came to visit"—except for his old friends, of course, and a few young writers who came for his advice. He loved the shack, and the forest and the sea and the birds so much that he resented people who reminded him of the hell that he saw "civilization" to be.

He would never have left the beach had he not been forced, and he wouldn't have stayed away had he been free to return. While he was there he was as content as a man could be whose soul was stretched and racked by opposites. Not all the tensions were negative, however—sometimes the extremes were equally attractive.

It was the Lowrys' winter custom to leave the beach and take up residence "in town" while ice solidified the well, and frost split fire-wood into solid chunks, and the northeasterlies slashed through the cracks around windows and doors. Margerie particularly suffered, for it was she who did most of the chores indoors and out. Malcolm left reluctantly, for during the absences there were committed many acts of petty vandalism: boulders were dumped into the well; windows were broken; occasionally there were forced entries and minor theft; and inevitably—by "Bad spirits" Malcolm used to say—the outhouse was twisted askew, or knocked over. Despite Old Jim's best efforts to prevent damage—he would come over every other day or so—the

Dorothy Jean Burt and Lowry on the Dollarton beach. (Special Collections Library, U.B.C., BC 1770/3.)

shacks needed steady occupancy to be totally secure, and Malc was never happy away from the beach.

Consequently, the homecoming in March or early April always had the air of carnival about it – a lightness of mood, pointless grins, sudden laughter – and all this in the knowledge that there would be damage to repair. The return of '53 is particularly memorable, for I never before or after heard anyone laugh so hard or so long as Malcolm did that day – and at his own jokes! Driving back from town I had told them that the outhouse had been put on its side, so it was no surprise when we reached the trail leading down the bank to the beach to see the massive, heavy-planked two-holer sagged on its side amongst the salmon-berry bushes, its great catch-pit gaping obscenely up at the trees. We took the suitcases down to the house, fortified ourselves with gin, and clambered up the stairs to start work.

As we approached the pit, Malcolm noisily cleared his throat, advanced to the edge of the hole, looked down, put his left hand to his heart and extended the right, and in the most perfectly resonant parody of melodrama declared, "O pardon me, thou bleeding piece of earth..." [*Julius Caesar*] at which point we both exploded in guffaws. The forest echoed with our hoots and sobs. Cheeks were soaked with tears. Throats were strained, sides aching. We staggered, bent over with hands on knees, grabbed trees, stumps, branches for support. Dorothy and Margerie came rushing to investigate, and they began to laugh. The noise would wane, then someone would look at someone else, and the groans would begin again, weaker, more painful, but continuing. We must have reacted for half an hour to that remark, and in the whole time not another word was spoken.

Finally, we went below for another gin, then returned to right the outhouse. Because Malc was not mechanically inclined—was, in fact, quite inefficient—I organized the operation, using block and tackle, and a cedar pole for a pry. The main problem was the weight of the structure, and its general lack of rigidity: many of the planks were half rotten, and were consequently heavy with water. Even the internal braces were rotting away, they had been there so long. (Malc told us later the place was dear to him: he had built it himself, and had read the whole of *Remembrance of Things Past* on its throne.) Together, we pried it up to a forty-five degree angle, and secured it. Then we put a line around the top, passed the line through the block, and began to heave. Slowly the great house came closer to the vertical. Malcolm was visibly excited, putting the whole force of his great frame into the heave on the line. I explained that there was a real danger that the house would fall in the opposite direction if we did not steady it when it came to the vertical, for we did not have enough line to make it fast. Malcolm nodded his understanding, and gave a prodigious tug on the line. The house tottered to the upright position, then began to lean and sag toward us. Malc lunged forward, braced himself with arms extended against side, and pushed with all force. I shot forward too, strained with all my might, and together we shoved the house back to vertical, where we were able to hold it with tackle this time. For a moment it had looked as though the house would topple over onto Malc, and both of us were alarmed and exhausted. He looked at me, grinned, and said, "Harvey, can you imagine what it would look like in the books to have the most famous Canadian author killed by a falling shithouse!" Again the guffaws, again the groans of laughter— Malcolm at his Rabelaisian best. And with it, a heavy labour was a joy.

There was the other side too, the completely innocent child. One example to illustrate this quality is particularly memorable, for it occurred not long after the homecoming described above. It happened that three birthdays fell within a ten-day period in July: Margerie's on the eighteenth, Dorothy's on the twenty-first, and Malcolm's on the twenty-eighth. Each was excuse enough for "a couple of drinks" to go with the greetings. Old Jim, the Lowrys' most-relied-on friend on the beach, was invariably present, for he would be invited to supper on the eighteenth and twenty-eighth. Somehow, Malcolm's day always developed into the longest and loudest of the celebrations, though on this occasion it began quite differently.

During the spring and summer of 'fifty-three I had been working with a professional puppeteer, and had acquired two three-foot marionettes as part payment. One was a tuxedo-dressed bald

Lowry in the summer of 1945. (Special Collections Library, U.B.C., BC 1614/8.)

Englishman called Mr. Plumley; the other was a black zoot-suiter called Dapper Dan. On Malcolm's birthday we used the marionettes to carry the presents. When we got to the shack the party had already begun—there was such noise—so Dorothy went in to make sure Malcolm would be sitting as far from the door as possible. Then she called us in.

First came Mr. Plumley, carrying a wrapped package of Player's cigarettes. As he stepped inside the door, the room became absolutely still. He introduced himself, bowed, minced across the room with his gift, and extended his right hand. Malcolm leaned forward, agog. With great charm and great delicacy, he took the hand between forefinger and thumb, and said how delighted he was at the meeting. Then Mr. Plumley said he had a friend outside who would like to meet "Mistuh Lowreh," and excused himself. He accepted being hung in a corner while I fetched the friend.

Dapper came in rather heavily—with a bottle of Bols gin wired to his left hand—and apologized for being late. Then he dragged the bottle across the room, singing "Happy Birthday" as he went. He finished the song about three feet from Malcolm's chair, and did a full bow. Malcolm was enthralled. He got out of his chair, knelt in front of the marionette, and extended his hand—first, this time. "How do you do, Dapper,"—very formal, as though to baron or earl. "I'm glad you were able to be with us." He continued the small-talk, still kneeling, and refused to try to work the control. He didn't take his eyes from Dapper Dan for a very long time.

With the additional gin the party progressed, and Dapper was placed—sitting upright—in a corner of the couch to observe the merry-making. Old Jim recited poems learned before the turn of the century in the Isle of Man. Somebody sang. Margerie taught Dapper Dan to sing "Parson Brown," to which Malcolm banged an accompaniment on his guitar. The noise level increased, and conversation went every which way. Several times Malcolm sat on the couch beside Dapper and held a long quiet dialogue with him. What they said no one heard, but there was obviously the full understanding of a child talking to his favorite doll.

When we left, Mr. Plumley was rolled up and put into his bag, but Dapper walked out with the rest of us. Malcolm followed us to the door and waved goodnight, not to the three humans, but to Dapper. I believe he never forgot that night, for many times after, even in Europe, he asked about Dapper Dan, and wished him good health. That is how children are with puppet friends they have made.

———————

Harvey Burt (b. 1920) is a retired school teacher. He and his wife Dorothy (b. 1908) live in the Deep Cove area of North Vancouver, close to the Dollarton beach.

"We Read One Another's Poetry"

In the early 1950s Curt Lang formed a friendship with the Canadian writer and poet Al Purdy, based on shared interests in poetry and literature. Lang was also friends with his high school French teacher, Downie Kirk. Through Kirk, Lang and Purdy were introduced to Lowry and they visited the Dollarton shack several times in 1953 and 1954. In 1957 Lowry wrote the Canadian writer and poet Ralph Gustafson, who was editing *The Penguin Book of Canadian Verse*, suggesting that Gustafson consider the works of "two wild western poets," Curt Lang and "Al somebody or other." Lowry stated that Lang "impressed me mightily as being a type I thought extinct: namely all poet, whose function is to write poetry... [and] I do think he is worthy of inclusion, even if you have to kick me out, for he is a young bloke who could use and deserves that kind of encouragement.... [H]e might well have genius" (*Selected Letters*, 409). (Gustafson received Lang's poems too late for inclusion in the anthology.) The following recollections are taken from an interview with Lang in May 1985:

> We all enjoyed each other's company. Malcolm's humour was a constant undercurrent. The English are noted for irony, for constantly mocking themselves and everything else; he was one of those and I found it amusing.
>
> Malcolm wasn't a great musician but he fancied himself as. He listened to jazz, played the ukulele quite badly, and sang pretty tunelessly, but it was fun. He thought he had written a Canadian national anthem but he was so drunk when he sang it that the rhythm was very harsh. I could get the intent: he was trying to evoke what he saw as the harshness of the country.
>
> We read one another's poetry but I didn't feel particularly taken to by Lowry; there was no sense of paternality. Lowry was a working writer and he was aware of his reputation and getting published. I was writing because I wanted to write, but I had no notion of writing for a career. I liked some poets and was influenced by them; I liked Al Purdy's poetry, and I liked Lowry's poetry very well. We would read our poetry to each other, enjoy it, show off and argue about it. For

instance, Lowry talked about the form of the sestina, but it wasn't like the practiced elder poet teaching the two rough-hewn westerners about this art. Malcolm was very proud of his mastery of the sestina. Whether you know the form or not it's beautiful because it imposes a very odd stricture on your thought. Words are rotated and repeated and this makes it dreamlike. We discussed it with considerable excitement and argument. We were all interested in the same things and glad for a chance to talk about them.

Malcolm was interested in what people thought, remembered, and said. In his writings he's constantly juxtaposing these, and usually with irony and horror. To someone who finds words meaningful, most people's use of words is shocking. I think Malcolm was shocked that way. You notice how he quotes from bits of songs and newspapers and things: "Sex fiend's tot feeds alligator," that was his version of a newspaper headline.

He was often critical of Vancouver in both his speech and writing. The way he described "Enochvilleport" in "The Bravest Boat" is quite savage and all true. One of the things that struck him as terrifying was the industry, the shipyards and sawmills. From Dollarton you can see the cracking tower across at Shellburn. Malcolm could evoke things through his speech and his writing, and although he was often geographically inaccurate, he was accurate in spirit. He wrote a poem about Hastings Street in which he described the faces of the drunks.[33] It was true. The faces of the people in Skid Road were terrifying. It was the one part of town where you would see that particular horror on people's faces: anguish, fury, despair. He's the only person I ever knew who wrote about it and evoked it.

I didn't see Malcolm as an overly sensitive, suffering soul as some people have portrayed him. Perhaps those comments were made in talking about his drinking, or perhaps the people making the comments imagined they knew him from reading about the Consul. I saw a TV show that depicted him that way and I thought, "That's an odd interpretation," because he has — had — such strong abilities. There are people for whom language evokes the world, and he was one of those. That's a powerful skill so he certainly didn't seem weak.

I found Malcolm ordinary for our set. I think I thought of myself and all my friends as extraordinary because what was of interest, what was real or ordinary to us, was not what was real or ordinary to other people. Malcolm was very strong-minded. He knew what he felt about things but he wasn't very practical about how to survive. He committed himself to what he was feeling when he was writing and he burned himself up. He did drink, which was self-destructive, and he reacted strongly to his experiences, but to say he was a pitiful, tortured soul strikes me as inappropriate.

We sometimes drank to unconsciousness. Margerie drank with us. She enjoyed it. What can I say? I'm sure that as a woman she would

The Lowrys' sundeck and pier at high tide, winter 1950. (Special Collections Library, U.B.C., BC 1614/113.)

have had misgivings between times. It's difficult to keep a house in order and party a lot. But we were all rather innocent about this and, drunk or sober, we felt we had infinite time and space. I know from their letters from England that she became concerned with Malcolm's health because she had to nurse him through the hangovers and she came to know the effect it had on him. But we all drank together then, gin and Seven-Up; it's quite tasty you know.

I have vivid recollections of our visits in Dollarton. Some of the houses along the water in Dollarton had log and plank floats in front, but the tide went by the Lowrys' place quite fast, so instead of a float they had made a little jetty on homemade pilings that went from the house to the water. At high tide you could bring a boat up to it, but at low tide it was dry. There's a big tidal difference in B.C.; I think seventeen feet at the maximum. We would be there all day, talking, eating, drinking, and during that time the tide would be up and down two or three times. When the tide was up you could walk out to the end of the jetty and there would be fifteen feet of salt water flowing two feet below the planks; if you jumped off when the tide was down, you'd land on your head on a rock.

I remember once when we were all cheerfully stoned, Malcolm appeared among us in his shorts and thundered off the end of the jetty into the chuck. The water's cold here, but he was strong and energetic. He'd swim around and yell, then he'd come blowing and puffing and struggling up against the current and climb up the ladder back onto the jetty. When the feeling of satisfaction would die down somebody else would jump in and do the same thing all over again.

We drank gin out of little peanut butter glasses with tulips on them. There was a brand of peanut butter that you bought in the supermarket and it came in a drinking glass so you not only got the peanut butter; when you were finished the peanut butter you had a drinking glass. They were thoughtful enough not to print the label on the glass; they put the label on the lid which you could throw away. Then you had a respectable, smallish drinking glass with little red tulips painted all over it. These would be fairly common household equipment at that time. That day a lot of jelly fish were going by in the tide. I remember finishing my gin and lying on my stomach on the jetty, catching jelly fish in gin glasses and passing them back for the others to admire. Everyone had a gin glass with a live jelly fish gyrating around in it.

I guess if you considered yourself an artist one of the things you didn't want to have, or made sure you didn't get stuck in, would be a steady job. Undoubtedly there are writers who have distinguished themselves in other professions while writing well, but I think Malcolm felt himself well out of that. Some have looked at his life and said he was unhappy because of a lack of success and recognition, but he was getting by. All of us were rather more pleased with our lives than not. I had no money and worked when I needed to, but I was young and life seemed easy in B.C. in those days. Purdy worked in a mattress factory and strongly resented the demands it made on his time and mind, but he had enough energy left to party and argue and write every evening and weekend.

In those days lots of people lived in cabins and shacks in B.C., but it was a luxury because they didn't have to pay rent or taxes. The Lowrys' shack had the basics. There was a primitive little kitchen; there were book shelves; there were several rooms: there was a bedroom; there was a nice living room with wooden window seats.[34] It wasn't fancy but it had a sense of freedom. They had all the firewood they wanted, it floated around for free. Lots of people in England live much worse.

Whether he was conscious of it or not, I think Malcolm would have felt this place refreshing after some of the places he'd been. The kinds of people that Malcolm met here were mostly English-speaking people with an interest in literature. In those days many people in Vancouver felt that freedom, that is freedom from boredom and drudgery, was more important than success; many saw Vancouver as a haven in that respect. I'd be careful not to go larger than life when you try to imagine those times.

Curt Lang (b. 1937) has worked on the Coast Steamship Lines, as a commercial fisherman and boatbuilder, and as a naval architect. He now works as a systems analyst and continues to write. He has lived in the Mediterranean, London, Montreal, and San Francisco, and now resides with his family in North Vancouver.

"This Fabulous Drunk"

The noted Canadian poet Al Purdy met Lowry through Curt Lang and Downie Kirk. Purdy's recollections of Lowry have appeared in two Canadian publications: *Books in Canada*, and *Canada Month*; as well as in Purdy's *No Other Country*. Extracts from these are reprinted with permission:

> Working in a Vancouver factory in 1954...I heard about this drunken novelist living in a squatter's shack on Burrard Inlet. Curt Lang, a 16 year-old who could talk the round collar off a theologian, assured me the guy was good. Downie Kirk...said the same.
>
> The three of us set out for the novelist's beach shack with two bottles of booze, of which I expected to consume more than my fair share. The shack was several miles away across the Second Narrows bridge, near Dollarton. Along the way Downie Kirk mentioned to Curt Lang and me that we might never get to meet this fabulous drunk at all. In a bad mood he might kick us unceremoniously off the property he didn't own. But the sun shone bright driving the shoreline road...we felt cheerful...[and] the novelist was in a good mood. Short, barrel-chested, with a red face, he received us cordially. We sat and drank and talked about nothing much all afternoon. His wife was more or less cordial too, a woman with cobweb wrinkles masking her face, as though the strain of living with her backwoods genius had aged her prematurely. Curt showed the novelist his poems, suitably impressing him. I felt left out, not having thought to bring poems, but resolved to remedy this later....The novelist...was more interested in drinking and talking about Haiti voodoo and firewalkers treading beds of hot coals with aplomb and composure. He also read one poem and we applauded his genius. I was impressed because the guy had actually been published, a *Good Housekeeping* certificate I found necessary to myself at the time.
>
> Near afternoon's end we had consumed the two bottles of booze we had brought and another that had been domiciled under the sink. The novelist and I set out for Vancouver to buy more, me driving my little English Prefect, hoping I looked sober. I wasn't, of course. At the liquor store near Main and Hastings the novelist bought six bottles of

Lowry holding a bottle of Bols Gin in 1953. (Special Collections Library, U.B.C., BC 1614/107.)

Bols gin. Then he told me there was [a] church with beautiful windows near by. We set out to look at the beautiful windows. A wedding was in process at the church. An authoritative clerical person was receiving wedding guests, but did not receive the novelist or myself with any warmth. I talked to the clerical person myself, feeling I looked the more respectable and certainly the less drunk. Then some wedding guests pulled up to the curb; the round collar turned to receive them. I turned to the novelist thinking here was our chance. But he was gone, already inside. When I caught up with him he was kneeling on the floor between long hardwood benches, six bottles of Bols gin in a brown grocery bag on the seat behind him.

Again I was impressed. Even with hindsight aiding foresight I don't know why. But the Ancient Mariner, with an albatross of booze around his neck, comes to mind. The red-faced novelist seemed to me a driven man, driven by devils in his own mind that shrieked in his ears and would not be stilled by anything but Bols gin. He fascinated me. Before driving back across the Second Narrows, I showed the novelist my own poems. He read them like a famous man and said little.[35]

On our second visit to the beach shack, the dead man [Lowry] went swimming in Burrard Inlet, his red face and barrel chest bobbing around in the cold water like pieces of coloured driftwood. Later, it seemed completely natural that my friend and I, Lowry and his wife, drank Bols gin, which sometimes replaced coffee and tea in that household.

It grew darker then. Across black water silver candles of the oil refinery lit the early evening, the same ones Lowry called, ironically, "the loveliest of oil refineries." He and my friend sang songs outside, while I sat at Lowry's typewriter and copied his poems by lamplight, feeling very literary and virtuous.

They were odd, doom-laden poems, very regular and formal, maybe even Elizabethan-sounding, death implicit in all of them. But in each poem, generally at the end, a line or two would silently go "boom": a phrase incandescent —

No Kraken shall depart till bade by name,
No peace but that must pay full toll to hell.

Then the rough-tender voices of my friends, the literary drunks, floated through the window to join in my mind the many-tentacled Kraken:

"Away, away, away you rolling river."[36]

But it was a long evening. Lowry recited his *Sestina in a Cantina*— his thespian voice bearing the full weight of archaic fear and horror; how the world is a great prison ruled by tossing mooseheads and witch doctors in business suits... Then he told the story of how A.J.M. Smith, the eminent critic, jumped out the front window at high tide fully clothed, apparently in a fit of euphoria induced by salt water and Bols gin. Lowry talked about the weird sorcerers of Central America, their seeming imperviousness to red hot coals, how sailors all seem to be part mystic and...

Falling silent he stared in front of him, as if the room was completely empty. Perhaps he was thinking of the tossing mooseheads that ruled the world? Or the match spurt of distant flame on its lone, swan-like steel neck at an oil refinery across the inlet? Of ships that sailed forever, revisiting the old ports over and over again, with bells clanging out the time, but no one ever knowing what time it is or was....

Time to go home. My friend is now extremely drunk. They invite us to stay the night but he will not....Lowry himself is also under the weather. Margerie has to guide us up the half-mile forest path to the highway. She doesn't want to very much, but thinks we'll get lost if she doesn't. I have to support my friend, half carry him up the dark trail. . . . Margerie with a flashlight hurrying ahead of us, afraid of mountain lions; myself with a drunken friend draped across my shoulders, laboring up the dark, steep trail. At the highway before Margerie turns to go back she asks curiously, "Are you two homosexuals?" I don't know whether I laughed or not.

Several months later, after the Lowrys had departed for Europe, I returned to the beach shack with my friend and a beautiful girl. We brought along a bottle of wine and drank it on the road, regaling the girl with tales of Lowry, about the savage mountain lions in that dark forest, striving to impress on her what a genius each one of us was. At the end of Lowry's dock we poured what remained of the wine into the sea, accompanied by a suitable oration. All were impressed with the literary solemnity of the moment. But I think that Lowry himself never made such gestures. He was always himself, whoever that strange person may have been.[37]

Al Purdy (b. 1918) began travelling and writing in his youth. In 1944 his first book of poems was published; in 1965 he won the Governor General's Award for poetry for *The Cariboo Horses*; he has written more than two dozen poetry collections and has edited a number of others. Purdy has written two poems on Lowry: "About Pablum, Teachers, And Malcolm Lowry" (*The Crafte So Longe to Learne*) and "Malcolm Lowry" (*The Cariboo Horses*). Purdy lives at Roblin Lake, Ameliasburg, Ontario, and continues to travel and write.

"A Great Deal of Love for Life"

William McConnell was a law student at the University of B.C. when Earle Birney introduced him to Lowry in 1947. McConnell and his wife Alice became close friends of Malcolm and Margerie. Writers themselves, the McConnells shared literary interests with the Lowrys, as well as a fondness for hiking and the outdoors.

Lowry's writing regimen, as well as McConnell's studies, his freelance work for the C.B.C., and, later, the demands of his law practice, kept them from visiting regularly. However, the quality of their time together compensated for the quantity. Correspondence between the Lowrys and the McConnells indicates their shared empathy:

May 24 [1952]

Dear Bill and Alice—

What ho?
Did you think we'd died, or faded away into the fourth dimension, or just abandoned life, liberty and the pursuit of happiness? Well, we nearly did. Please forgive us for being such droops. Malcolm has been having a long beastly siege over his contract.... Now I wish to god I could say—come at once. But poor Malc was just unable to work properly... and has just now recovered and begun to organize himself, and until such time as he gets *inside* his work again he simply cannot disorient himself, even for a day. This particularly trying stage, of having lost touch with what he was doing, shouldn't last very long, and just as soon as he's got control of his work again we're looking forward to... having a gorgeous day bird watching. I'm holding our too-long awaited visit to you in front of our noses like a carrot.... Meantime, please forgive us for our silence. I know you understand, that's one of the nicest things about you, that you *do* understand... We may be erratic friends, but we love you. God bless....

Love from us both,
Margerie (U.B.C. 3:4)

June 12/52.

Dear Malcolm & Margerie:

Bless both of you! No, we knew you hadn't died or abandoned life, but naturally and happily assumed that you were having a siege with publishers and proofs.... Hell, both of you make such inordinate demands on your selves for your writing (as one should and must) that a mere month or two delay in seeing us is perfectly understandable, justifiable, natural and laudable.... There's nothing erratic about your discipline to your work. We admire and respect it (and wish to God we had some more of it ourselves).... We're all well... though I'm tired from a long sludge of work during the past three months.... Oxford Press is bringing out an anthology in the autumn with one of my radio stories in it; contract was even a fair one.... Most of the ducks have gone north but there are a few young families still here. The three cherry trees which shade our cottage are a haven for finches and song sparrows. The Great Blue Herons from your North Arm heronry [Map 3] still spend their days standing patiently in the marsh....

> Love to you both
> Bill (U.B.C. 1:46)

The McConnells' son Arthur also had a special bond with the Lowrys. Although they are brief, Arthur's memories are "vivid." As of 1985, his are the only recollections of Lowry in adulthood to be recorded from the point of view of a child. In a letter written to the author in September 1985, Arthur recalls:

They were both friendly and warm and there was always a sense of occasion when they visited our cottage in Burnaby or we visited them in Dollarton; much laughter as well as serious conversation. I had a sense of comradeship with both of them, but with Malcolm in particular.

My strongest impression of Malcolm was of great gentleness that seemed to conflict with his powerful muscular presence. I think children quickly recognize extreme sensitivity in older people and I found kindness, generosity, and shyness strongly evident in his character.

Malcolm enjoyed hearing about my enthusiasm for music and the violin. He would ask many questions and would listen carefully to my answers. I don't recall playing the violin for him but am sure I did as this was a regular event when we had guests.

Malcolm would read some of his writing to my parents and Margerie and hours of discussion would follow. I would usually sit fascinated by the exchange of ideas even if I didn't understand the content of what was being said.

We often visited the shack at Dollarton and it was always an enjoyable adventure. Dad would ask Malcolm if he'd been swimming to-day and I remember him pointing across [Burrard Inlet] and commenting that Malcolm swam to the other side and back again every day. It was probably a mile or so but seemed an incredible distance to my young eyes.

On one occasion I remember seeing what I thought was a banjo hanging on the wall of their home.[38] I asked my mother who played it. She said that Malcolm did....He strummed it and showed me some simple chords which kept me occupied for the afternoon. On other occasions I would walk beside my father and Malcolm, either on the beach or in the forest, and listen to them involved in conversation. I could sense how much my father enjoyed talking with Malcolm.

I was very conscious that Malcolm was regarded by those who knew him as someone special. I had heard him called a "genius" many times.... I had overheard stories from my parents' friends...about his drinking bouts but I can not recall him behaving in any way other than a gentleman. It was always a pleasure to be with Malcolm as he was so nice and seemingly unaffected by his talent. We had days and evenings of great warmth, good humour, and discussion.

We often received post cards from Malcolm after he left Vancouver and I recall his unusually tiny writing. I clearly remember hearing of his death: there was great sorrow in our family and I was also aware that a great artist had died.

The bond between Lowry and McConnell was special, and they were "not afraid of silences, which sometimes were more important than conversation."[39] After Lowry's death, Margerie turned to the McConnells for solace and continued to visit and correspond with them until deteriorating health prevented her from doing so. According to McConnell, both he and Alice helped Margerie to edit a number of Lowry's posthumously published works, including "The Forest Path to the Spring" and *October Ferry to Gabriola*; McConnell is acknowledged for the assistance he gave Lowry regarding the "legal matters" in *October Ferry*, and for suggesting to Margerie the title *Psalms and Songs* for a selection of Lowry's short stories, with reminiscences and criticism.

The following recollections are taken from interviews with William McConnell conducted in November 1984 and January 1985:

Malcolm was a very shy man, especially at social gatherings: with more than two or three people he'd be very reticent and found it difficult to cope. One evening I took the Lowrys to a Shakespearean play and although he professed to enjoy the play very much, Malcolm sweated right through it. We were sitting in the middle of the theatre and I realized that the presence of all the people around him was just too much. Margerie later told me that they always got aisle seats when they went to the movies.

On another occasion he was unwisely invited to a house party. He thought he was being exploited and got horribly drunk.... Malcolm had a tremendous amount of innocence to his character. He was easily hurt; if he felt slighted in any way he would try to hide it, but it would be obvious. I don't think most people knew how painfully shy and sensitive he was, but I think it explains, in part, his drinking while attending gatherings. He always wrote the most marvellous letters of apology to his host or hostess after such events. His alcoholic phases have been overstressed in the films and in a lot of the criticism and commentary about Malcolm. He's portrayed as a person who was always drinking; that's not true. He often went months and months without taking a drink. I know, from Margerie, he didn't take a drink for six months when he was re-doing the manuscript of *Under the Volcano* at Niagara-on-the-Lake, even though they were living in a vineyard at the time, and their host was making wine.

Although Margerie wore blue jean type clothing around the shack, she was always well dressed when they went out, as was Malcolm. He was a very neat, fastidious person and when they visited you they dressed up. Visiting was a social event for them and they were both punctilious in that respect. With us they were a very generous couple, intellectually and socially. We spent much of our time together reading our writings to each other and discussing literature, music, art, and law.

We visited the shack as often as I could possibly manage with my busy professional life at the time. In turn, they visited our home quite often and would bring armloads of prize jazz recordings from Malcolm's collection, as well as recent manuscripts to read. They didn't have a car, so we would drive over and get them, usually in the morning, and they'd spend the whole day with us. I recall one beautiful spring Saturday when we played his records, drank wine, danced, the doors were open, the fruit trees were in bloom, and it was just a perfect day, a wonderful day; one of quite a few that we had together.

We were living at Burnaby Lake, which was a wild bird sanctuary, at the time. Both Malcolm and Margerie were great bird watchers. They had an encyclopedic knowledge of birds: sea birds, shore birds, and mountain birds. In this zone they could view all three types, which they did with great excitement. As a result, my wife and I became bird watchers ourselves.

Malcolm was a great practical joker on an intellectual plane. He had a great sense of humour and a tremendous baritone barrel of laughter. He loved the absurd and bellowed with enjoyment if I told him a scandalous story from the courts. He loved the anomalies of law, which he considered to be the anomalies of fiction or life itself.

We didn't see the dark side of Malcolm. He was always on his best behaviour with us and I think this was because of our son Arthur, who was fairly young at the time. Arthur was a violinist, having started at the age of four, and he and Malcolm shared a passionate interest in music. Malcolm would make a pact with my son that he would play his jazz recordings if Arthur would play the violin later. Malcolm was patient with Arthur and never talked down to him; they talked together like adults. He treated children as if they were grown up and children responded to that. Malcolm was also a physical person so there was a lot of scuffling around with a soccer ball, which small boys enjoy. Arthur thought Malcolm was a wonderful person.

Malcolm was a short man, tremendously broad and powerfully built. He had hands that were very delicate and small for the rest of his body, but the first time he shook hands with me he nearly broke my hand. He had very very blue, clear eyes and his gaze was most penetrating. He seemed to not only stare into your eyes but also into your thoughts.

Malcolm had a beautiful voice; one might term it a mellifluous voice. He spoke clearly, distinctly, and very precisely—almost in paragraphs. He had a marvellous vocabulary and would always search for the exact word in conversation. As a result he appeared hesitant to some people, but it was just his thought processes. His mind was anything but hesitant. It was like a steel trap.

The other thing that I think was so impressive about Malcolm was his incredible memory. He would recall a conversation six months later to ask me to amplify some remark he or I had made. It wouldn't be a paraphrase, it would be the exact remark. He never seemed to forget anything. If I gave him a book to read he would quote whole paragraphs of the book verbatim. I think he really had a photographic memory.

Malcolm affected to be one of the common people, which was rather ludicrous because the man was an intellectual genius. I think he suffered because he saw so much more than us normal people. His perception was such that he could hardly bear it. He saw more meaning to what to me would be an ordinary instance of daily life: he would see perhaps half a dozen meanings in it, and he symbolized everything. He talked the way he wrote. There were many skeins in his conversation: quite a few levels at any one time. Often it would be several days before you'd perceive two or three of them. He was a man who caused you to think a great deal after a discussion. Malcolm had no intellectual pretensions whatsoever. He thought everybody else amongst his friends to be far brighter than he was.

I suspect that Malcolm suffered from feelings of inferiority and guilt, being what his older brother called a "remittance man." There was a certain amount of self-pity about that; also he felt he couldn't cope with daily life the same way that other people did. There was a commingled aspect of inner pity and self guilt in his personality.

Malcolm suffered in the way that I suppose every introspective artist suffers: he was unable to disgorge everything that he felt, sensed, read or knew intuitively. I think his suffering was of the universal suffering, but redeemed by his awareness that nothing is really lost, no energy is lost. He was not religious in the formal sense, but he was deeply religious in the real sense.

Another aspect of Malcolm that you don't hear much about is that he was tremendously generous intellectually. He never thought he was a great writer, it was always the other person. He was tremendously curious about what I was doing, both professionally and as a writer.

My wife and I shared some of our writings with the Lowrys; all their friends did, at Malcolm's request. He would get very excited, no matter how poor it was.

Malcolm would read us his work, first draft, except it was never first draft: he was constantly adding and changing even when he was reading. He'd listen very carefully for comments; he welcomed criticism. Listening to Malcolm read was absolutely wonderful. As I said he had a beautiful voice and he never slurred a word. He would usually pace up and down, reading perfectly even though he was interpolating and adding while he was reading. He would jot down notes or additions on anything that was handy, including cigarette papers. He read us the first draft of *October Ferry* at one sitting. He started about 2:30 or 3:00 in the afternoon and ended in the early morning hours. I had to leave the room out of necessity around midnight and he looked up, stopped his reading, and said, "Don't you like my prose?"

We had long discussions about writing. I loaned him all of T.E. Lawrence's work, which he didn't know, and he fell under the spell of Lawrence. He'd had a classical education at Cambridge...but Malcolm had surprising gaps in his reading, surprising in that he was a compulsive and an impulsive reader. He would read the small print on bus transfers, for example, and the little brochures that the electric company sent out with their hydro bills. He would even read Wrigley's gum labels, on all sides, including the ingredients. I suppose like all good writers he was a compulsive collector of useless information — which turned up in his fiction over and over again.

Malcolm didn't think he was a great writer, he just loved writing as he loved reading. It would be a shock to Malcolm to be regarded as a great writer. He just thought he was doing a job and doing it as best he could. Hence his constant rewriting and his overwriting.

He had no sense of proportion. I remember him telling me how he was going to win a $500.00 prize put out by the Royal Bank, who used to run a double page ad in *Maclean's* magazine called "We Printed This Because We Liked It." It was to be 500 words, if I recall, but he couldn't stop writing and ended up with approximately 350 pages.[40]

Apart from the dozen or so writers in Vancouver, at the time, Malcolm wasn't acclaimed as a great writer when the *Volcano* first came out. And when he died I recall the C.B.C. phoning me from Toronto and asking if I had a copy of *Under the Volcano* because the Toronto Public Library didn't have one. By that time it had been translated into twenty-two or twenty-three languages! A familiar Canadian story. He received more acclaim in Europe, particularly France, then he did in Canada and he was lionized in, of all places, Cuba and Haiti.

Margerie had a very strong character. She was a practical person and a great support to Malcolm. She was a writer in her own genre and was probably Malcolm's best critic. Some people have suggested that Margerie did all the labour around the shack but that's an overstatement: if you saw Malcolm chopping wood on the beach it would give the lie to that.

Margerie was born in what is now known as Hollywood, but at that time was just ranch country. She was a champion horseback rider and acted in "oaters," cowboy movies in the early silent film days of Hollywood. I remember her telling me that when she was in films she had a pet cheetah. She'd leave the cheetah in the back seat of her convertible when she parked it to do her shopping, until the police department insisted that she could not take the cheetah into town with her. She was a gay person and had a flamboyant side to her character. It was easy to see how Malcolm fell completely in love with her. He worshipped Margerie throughout his life.

Margerie with a cat ("Nunki"?) on the Dollarton beach. (Special Collections Library, U.B.C., BC 1614/95.)
In one journal Margerie wrote:

> *A great log came drifting in one sunny morning with the tide. Malcolm was entranced with it & nothing would do but he must capture it and lay it at my feet. He towed it in & we struggled all day to get it anchored, making fine plans for building a pier....Now the creature lies there, stretching across our whole beach....So far it has defied all efforts to move it & lies there, sullenly beautiful & proudly defiant (U.B.C. 21:8).*

Malcolm and Margerie loved the natural beauty and seclusion of Dollarton, but there were aspects of Vancouver that they didn't like. For example, what we call beer parlours and what Malcolm referred to as our "hòrrible pubs." Living in Dollarton also caused them frustrations, especially the bus service which was only once or twice a day. They were both avid readers and they often walked into North Vancouver, across the bridge, and then took the bus to the public library [Vancouver's Carnegie Library—Map 1] to get books. Although they were both great walkers, it was a long walk. Another frustration, until *Volcano* was printed, was that they didn't know too many, shall we say, literate people in Vancouver. Not that there were a great number. I think the intellectual isolation until the late forties and early fifties must have been trying; they carried on an extensive correspondence with friends in other parts of North America.

They did come to have a good many friends in Vancouver whom they were very loyal to—friendship counted a great deal to them. Malcolm always insisted on walking us up the trail to the road. It was a steep difficult trail which at times went through a forest of very tall trees. At the top, when we got in our car, it was "God Bless." His letters and Christmas cards always contained the expression, "God Bless the McConnell household." That is also the inscription he wrote in our copy of *Under the Volcano*.

I think everything was a personal symbol for Malcolm, and in the case of the shack I would certainly underline that remark. Eviction was always preying on their minds and they were heartbroken about the possibility of losing their beloved shack. I doubt if he could have lived anywhere else because he and Margerie were so completely and utterly happy there.

They were worried that the whole landscape was going to change, as it did progressively with the population explosion which occurred after the Second World War. They were worried about the environment because the oil refineries were right opposite them and occasionally a tanker would have an oil spill. On one occasion Malcolm and I were walking on the beach and there was a seagull dead from oil. He was most concerned and most upset; again, it became a symbol. On another walk Malcolm waved his hand over the area, lamenting that it was all going to disappear, it was all going to be lost. To him that was personal loss and physical loss—not just a loss of a place to live, but a loss to the ecology with which he was very concerned.

Their shack was remarkably comfortable, with three rooms and a gorgeous view. However life in the shack was beset with problems and hardships. We went to Dollarton one wintry afternoon and their stove needed repairing. Malcolm had some clay from one of the banks along the beach. Being a cold day, the stove was filled with wood and was red hot. Malcolm was very very carefully, with his small sensitive hands, trying to fix a chink in the stove with this wet clay. He was repeatedly burning his fingers and cursing because the stove was far too hot, but he kept persisting, explaining that this was the only way the clay would dry.

All of life was a drama as far as Malcolm was concerned. Just getting their drinking water was an everyday adventure. They usually rowed the boat three or four hundred yards down the beach because it was much easier access than going through the thick, steep forest. They made a romance out of any misadventure. If a disaster occurred, like an extra high tide, they'd relate it as a marvellous anecdote two or three weeks later. I recall Malcolm recounting with glee how they had coped with a storm: at 3:00 in the morning he had gone out to stave off logs that the high tide was throwing up against the foundations of their shack.

They also dealt with life with a great deal of humour. An example is when Malcolm broke his leg: it was a very severe fracture, but he made an anecdote out of it and saw the funny side of it, even after spending several weeks in St. Paul's Hospital with serious surgery. It was a Roman Catholic Hospital and at that time most of the nurses were nuns. They wore a black cowl edged with white and he called them the "Cowled Sisters of Darkness." To Malcolm they were the antithesis of angels of mercy.

I saw him two months after his leg injury and he told me of his horror when the orthopedic surgeon had at first suggested that he might have to have his leg amputated. The surgeon turned and pointed to an artificial limb, ran his hand down it, and said, "Oh they make them almost as good as real now you know. They're classical." Without thinking I then told him about this classical criminal court case I had won. I said, "It was a classic, just classic." As I finished Malcolm reached over and stroked an imaginary leg and said, "A classical case. A classical case. You're just like my goddamn surgeon!"

Malcolm had an abiding fascination with the law and was always asking me about cases I had worked on, as well as various aspects of law. It was not just the fascination of a writer, it was also the fascination of a person concerned with the social fabric. He was horrified, for example, when I told him about the time lag between a social necessity or need and when the legislation would eventually occur. He thought Canadian law was arbitrary due to this time lag. He was also fascinated with the whole concept of law being inviolable, in the sense that both lawyers and judges were bound by it until the law was changed, either by precedent, which is a very slow process, or by legislation. The time lag, and what happened to people in the interim, really concerned him.

Malcolm was fascinated with the whole process of execution in Canada and elsewhere. He listened to a long program I prepared for the C.B.C. called "Capital Punishment: The Mind or the Heart." There had been an international sociological convention in Vancouver

Lowry in a leg cast in the summer of 1953. (Special Collections Library, U.B.C., BC 1614/110.)

and I had interviewed a number of the delegates, including the deputy warden of Sing Sing Prison, who had to supervise people going to the electric chair; Harry Richmond, the prison doctor at Vancouver's Oakalla Prison, who had to be present during every hanging; and the Minister of Justice for India who had a backlog of fifteen thousand individuals due for the hangman!

Like myself, Malcolm was strongly opposed to capital punishment. He felt that man was trying to play God and to some extent that was true. Capital punishment is based on tribal law and that is retribution. . . . It's a social condition which is more suitable for a society that cannot exercise much control. Malcolm was also fascinated with the fact that of all crimes, recidivism, that is repetition of the crime, occurs less in murder than in any other offence.

Malcolm knew that hanging was not the merciful death that it was portrayed to be. It's not instantaneous. It varies from person to person. Theoretically the hangman is supposed to be aware of the body weight etcetera, but everyone's metabolism is different. I know of one instance in which it took eighteen minutes for the person to be pronounced dead, that is legally dead; in another the person was not dying and the hangman provided the extra weight needed by pulling on the person's legs; in one case the head was actually severed from the body. Malcolm was aware of all this and some of the hangings he described in *October Ferry* are based on hangings which took place in Vancouver's Oakalla Prison; where, as in the novel, an unused elevator shaft was used to accommodate the scaffold.

I remember Malcolm discussing the case of the seventeen year old boy who was to be hung for murder in Vancouver in 1951.[41] Malcolm was bothered by the fixedness and immutability of the law: the boy's age didn't matter. Malcolm showed me a letter he wrote to the editor of one of the local newspapers in which he complained of this, but I don't know if it was ever printed.

After Malcolm's death I had to go to Europe for three months, on business. Margerie wrote and asked if I would interview Mrs. Mason, their landlady in Ripe. Up to that time Mrs. Mason had refused to be interviewed, but consented when asked by Margerie....I had a marvellous B.B.C. technician who did the impossible, a half hour interview in one take....Unfortunately, the tape was lost between B.B.C. London and C.B.C. Ontario.

From my notes, and what I personally recall, Mrs. Mason thought that Malcolm and Margerie were very happy....He was working on revising the short stories, and two nights before Malcolm died they were busy with their ordnance maps of the Lake District. He was describing to Margerie exactly where they would stop for the night on the walking tour they intended to take.[42]

Malcolm had been in a so-called clinic in London five or six months beforehand....He had been sober for months...and was taking the prescribed anti-depressant pills....Mrs. Mason was convinced that Malcolm's death was not a suicide and that was borne out by the jury's verdict which was "Death by Misadventure." "Misadventure" is a legal term and is an indication of inadvertence, not intention: such as combining alcohol and anti-depressant or sleeping pills.

Malcolm was definitely not the type of person who would take his own life. In the radio program which I produced for the C.B.C.,[43] shortly after Malcolm's death, this point was made loud and clear by his Vancouver friends, particularly Earle Birney. Malcolm was, as Earle put it, "not a quitter." He never quit anything.

Malcolm had a great deal of love for life. He was not a

self-destructive individual. This is a popular misconception, unfortunately induced to some extent by the "official biography." Most of the time Malcolm was very hard working, extremely jolly, very happy, and very constructive in his outlook. He did have bleak periods, but they didn't last that long. His body of work shows this; not only his body of work but also his incredible amount of editing, rewriting, rewriting. I've never seen the equal of it. He was never finished with a manuscript, never. I think part of his problems before he died were due to the terrible worry hanging over him as to where were they going to find a harbour, where were they going to find the peace that they'd had in Dollarton?

Arthur McConnell (b. 1944) studied at the Royal Academy of Music in London and won many awards, including the Commonwealth Prize. In 1966 he studied under Ivan Galamian in New York; returned to England in 1972 and was engaged as a violinist with the Royal Philharmonic and other major orchestras. He now lives with his family in Wales and is Senior Lecturer and Head of String Studies at the Welsh College of Music and Drama.

William McConnell (b. 1917) has been writing and publishing since 1939. He graduated from the University of B.C. and practiced law in the Vancouver area until his recent retirement. In the 1940s and 1950s McConnell and his wife Alice (1913 – 1982) wrote a number of stories for the C.B.C. radio program "Anthology." He has published stories in several Canadian magazines and anthologies, and his article "Recollections of Malcolm Lowry" was published in *Canadian Literature* 6 (Autumn, 1960): 24 – 30; *Masks of Fiction: Canadian Writers on Canadian Prose*, edited by A.J.M. Smith and Malcolm Ross (1961), pp. 141 – 150; and *Malcolm Lowry: The Man And His Work*, edited by George Woodcock (1971), pp. 154 – 162. McConnell is the editor of Klanak Press and has known and befriended many Canadian literary figures.

Conclusion

In 1954 the District of North Vancouver was making preparations to develop Cates Park, and public pressure was mounting to have the shacks removed. The squatters slowly began abandoning their beach homes. George Meckling, an engineer for the District of North Vancouver, was given the job of "disposing of the...illegal structures on the beach."[1] He recalls that demolition of the shacks was started in 1954 and that there were only thirty to forty left in 1955 when he began working for the District:

> Our department would go out and talk to...[the squatters] and tell them that we had instructions to clean...[the beach] up....They began to realize that the municipality meant business this time....I was doing it in a gentlemanly fashion...but would just keep pickin' at 'em....Finally one person would move and soon as they moved we'd be there the next day with a bulldozer and flatten it and burn it....The down and out shacks were the last...but they finally moved too....Not, perhaps, because of our pressure but by the fact that they were getting some very adverse publicity.

According to Meckling, the last shacks were destroyed late in 1958. The park was left undeveloped for a few years because other areas of the District were growing more rapidly. It was not until the latter part of the 1960s that the Dollarton area had grown sufficiently to warrant the park's development.

A notice of eviction, the approaching cold of winter, concerns for Margerie's health, and an impending one thousand dollar income tax debt forced the Lowrys to abandon their "beloved shack."[2] In August 1954 they left Dollarton, but Lowry never gave up hope of returning and recapturing the vitality and happiness he had found there.

From the time of their departure, Lowry and Margerie lived in a state of physical and emotional upheaval. As in the past, when he was removed from his Burrard Inlet environment, Lowry began to drink heavily; his health waned, resulting in numerous hospitalizations. This time, however, there was to be no return to Dollarton and no "general recovery."

In their quest for a new home the Lowrys travelled to Italy. Shortly after their arrival in Milan, Lowry began vomiting blood and was hospitalized for a week.[3] They then moved to Taormina,

Sicily, but Lowry found that not even the beauty of the Mediterranean could relieve his despondency and sense of loss. In a letter written'from Taormina (to Giorgio and Daniela Monicelli) he stated:

> All has so far been anything but heavenly with us, largely due to my own ghastly incapacity to look my own grief in the face which, not liking not to be looked at, becomes all the greater each time I fail (U.B.C. 3:9).

Lowry also complained of the attitudes of the Sicilians who gave him "hypocrite lectures. . . about drinking their bloody wine even at the moment I am being overcharged for it" (U.B.C. 3:9). Added to this, the lack of seclusion and his pining for Dollarton made it difficult for him to write. In April 1955 Margerie wrote Lowry's editor Albert Erskine:

> Sicily was a mistake. . . but. . . we couldn't leave, first because we didn't have the money, and then we'd got involved with a house, etc. . . . Neither Malc or I have been able to do much work here—the *noise* has nearly driven us crazy. And Malc, of course cannot be driven to work (in that case he just gets frantic and *can't* work) nor can he be led, (he just gets balky and blank). In short, God help us, he has to do it himself, in his own way, in his own time. . . . When he tried despite noise to get down to *Gabriola*, he found it still too immediately and personally anguishing. . . . However it is there, and one day you'll have it, and it will be terrific. I think if we manage to settle in England for a year or so he'll whip it into shape before long. Of course, when he found he couldn't work on *Gabriola*, he was sure he'd lost his genius, would never be able to write again, etc. . . . So we've had a bit of a whingding, but as. . . he's calming down now, and with the decision to leave here (God, how he hates it!) he's feeling better too (U.B.C. 51:5).

In June 1955 the Lowrys moved to England, where they spent two months "drifting about from one London hotel to another."[4] Lowry's alcoholism and mental health were worsening, and in September 1955 he was voluntarily admitted to Brook General Hospital. In a letter to their friend David Markson (26 September 1955), Margerie said that Lowry "could no longer write—even a letter," and "was increasingly losing any contact with reality" (U.B.C. 51:5). At first it was thought he might need to have a lobotomy, but after a rest of close to two months, Margerie wrote Markson:

The magnificent old boy has done it again. Pulled himself together, God knows how, & they've *definitely* decided against any operation.... He will never be "normal" but his genius is intact, memory still phenomenal & his wit & sense of humour is now in great form. You should hear his descriptions of the horrors in his ward (U.B.C. 51:5).

However, after his discharge Lowry continued to drink, and in November 1955 was admitted to Atkinson Morley's, a psychiatric hospital; he was not released until February 1956. In that time he underwent analysis and electric shock treatments to relieve his depressed emotional state, as well as apomorphine aversion therapy in an attempt to cure his worsening alcoholism.[5] Margerie told Markson (14 January 1956) that Lowry would

need psychiatric care probably for the rest of his life...& will very likely have other blow-ups & muddles, even dangerous & sudden violent ones.... They are *sure* he'll be able to work again. Thank God. That, working, again, is part of his cure, in fact.... He'll *never* be able to travel...& must make up his mind to stay here for good.... He can *not* stand any excitement, or change of any sort again (U.B.C. 51:5).

After his discharge the Lowrys moved to a cottage in the small village of Ripe. Margerie called their new home a "dream house." Although the new surroundings did bring them a degree of peace and happiness, Lowry described it to Markson as a "temporary home" and wrote Jimmy Craige:

Please don't think we have abandoned Dollarton, we have not, and think of it constantly, and of yourself, and miss the old times, but it seems better for reasons of health to stay where we are just at the moment, though the beach will always be home (*Selected Letters*, 384).

Lowry's longing for Dollarton was so acute that the doctors at Atkinson Morley's recommended that he not work on *October Ferry to Gabriola* as it upset him emotionally.[6] He continued to drink heavily and in June 1956 was again admitted to Atkinson Morley's. When Lowry was discharged in August, Margerie's stamina was weakening. In 1955 she had been hospitalized for exhaustion; her emotional strength was again depleted and she had a nervous collapse. In October 1956 she was admitted to Luke's Woodside Hospital in London, where she rested under heavy sedation for more than a month. Concern for Margerie rallied Lowry and he wrote Markson that he was on "an absolute inconvertible wagon" of sobriety (*Selected Letters*, 389). He also promised her sister and brother-in-law, Priscilla and Bert Woolfan, that he would "absorb all shocks for her. . . good or bad": the good being that interest was being shown in their screenplay of *Tender is the Night*, and Lowry had received $500.00 for a six month film option on *Under the Volcano*; the bad being that of her mother's death (*Selected Letters*, 389 – 391). After Margerie's discharge they returned to Ripe, where Lowry cared for her during her home convalescence.

Since his departure from Dollarton, Lowry had written little other than letters. He now settled back into a writing routine and proceeded to work on his collection of short stories and what was to be his last novel, *October Ferry to Gabriola*. In a letter to Maria Moore of the Harold Matson Company, in January 1957, Margerie stated, "Malc is so completely immersed in his book he doesn't want to stop to even eat or sleep" (U.B.C. 51:6). As in the past, Lowry drew upon personal afflictions. *October Ferry* became "a huge and sad novel about Burrard Inlet" (*Selected Letters*, 409), in which the main character, Ethan Llewelyn, along with his wife, has to contend with the threat of eviction.

In April 1957 Lowry wrote that he and Margerie were planning on "going to live in the Lake District, in Grasmere, . . . because if we half shut our eyes we may be able to imagine we're back on Burrard Inlet!" (*Selected Letters*, 410). In June the Lowrys went on a walking tour of the Lake District and, as in Dollarton, birdwatched, picnicked, and boated. An entry in Lowry's "last notebook" compares the two locales and indicates a wistful yearning for the "brave pier" which had collapsed in 1956. He wrote:

> Impression that objects are trying to communicate to you with love: beyond limitations of country & time the pier in Grasmere trying to look like Dollarton. . . the buoy marker. . . trying to look like the head of a seal (U.B.C. 7:14).

Photographs taken during this time show Lowry looking sombre and lost to inner reflections. Passages in *October Ferry* poignantly express his sense of loss and the irreplaceability of "Eridanus":

> When he said they'd never find such a house as their cabin in a million years he really meant it. Ethan simply did not believe that the sort of

Lowry at Easedale Tarn, the Lake District, England, June 1957.
(Special Collections Library, U.B.C., BC 1614/123.)

conjunction of favoring yet opposing circumstances which had maintained Eridanus' existence in balance for so long could arise again, or be discovered elsewhere to have arisen. *Another* Eridanus was not to be found. Where else could you find the freedom, the privacy, the absolute privacy, and yet when you needed it, the friendliness, not too far, not too near, where else find all man's simple needs so simply satisfied.[7]

The events of the evening of 26 June 1957 are confused, but it is known that Lowry consumed a portion of a bottle of gin before arguing with Margerie, who smashed the bottle against a wall to prevent his finishing it. Margerie then left Lowry to his dinner and writing, and did not return to his room until early the next morning. When she entered, she found Lowry dead. A coroner's jury cited his death as the result of the combined effects of gin, barbituates, and inhalation of stomach contents — "Death by Misadventure."

Devastated, Margerie moved to Taormina, Sicily, where she could live inexpensively and where the hot, dry climate would aid her physical recuperation. After the winter she moved to California to be closer to her sister and brother-in-law, Priscilla and Bert Woolfan. From Taormina (October 1957), she wrote Earle and Esther Birney that

the full force of the terrible loneliness and grief has hit...and oh God how I wish I were dead too and lying beside him [Malcolm]....I suppose I have to pull myself together and do what I can about his work, but every time I...see his handwriting I simply have hysterics. I was always so close to it [his work], it was such an intimate integral part of our lives.

(Birney Papers, University of Toronto)

From the time of Lowry's death, Margerie has been involved with what she described as her "dreadful responsibility" and her "labour of love" (Birney Papers, University of Toronto), the sorting and editing, alone and with others, of a vast selection of Lowry's writings for posthumous publication.

In 1987, Margerie is eighty-two years old and in fragile health. Now living in Los Angeles, she is comforted by the companionship of her sister Priscilla, her friend Dr. Betty Moss (Ph.D.), and, undoubtedly, by her memories of "Malc" and the halcyon days in their "beloved shack."

Like Lowry, the squatters' shacks are gone and the once "primeval forest" near Roche Point is now Cates Park—a recreation site with paved roadways, a boat launch area, concession stand, life guards, and playgrounds. However, as Lowry himself wrote: "If one has to be threatened with eviction, to be threatened for the sake of a park is perhaps best."[8] Through Lowry's writings, as well as in the park setting, aspects of Burrard Inlet and the "favoring yet opposing circumstances" of the landscape have been preserved: the beach, the Shell refinery, the Roche Point light beacon "standing lonely on its cairn,"[9] the "halooing" of distant trains, deep sea vessels moving up and down the inlet, "seagulls blowing four ways at once," the wild cherry trees blooming in the spring, and at every full moon the pines writing "a Chinese poem on the moon."

Appendix 1

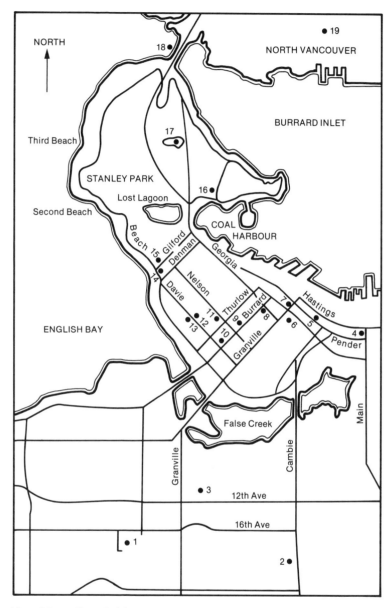

18. Lions Gate Bridge, one of two bridges linking Vancouver and North Vancouver. The Lowrys would have travelled over the bridge going between North Vancouver and Dollarton.

19. The site of the Heywood Park Auto-Camp (at Marine Drive and what was Keith Road). The Park still exists (1987) at Marine Drive and Hamilton – p. 34 – 5.

1.   Seymour Golf and Country Club: opened 1953 — p. 29.
2. = · = Dollar Road: built 1918; the top portion of the road is now called Fairway Drive.
3.   Dollar Mill (1916 – 1943) — p. 12.
4.   Vancouver Cedar Mill (1912(?) – 1929) — p. 12.
5.   Cates Park: recreation site that replaced the squatter community near Roche Point.
6.   □ Squatters' Shacks: 1930 – 1954.
7.   ■ Lowry's 2nd and 3rd Shack: approximate location — pp. 20, 28.
8.   Percy Cummins' General Store and Garage: where the Lowrys purchased their groceries, sometimes hauled water from Percy's tap, caught the bus, received their mail, and used Percy's telephone. The garage building still exists in 1987.
9.   McKenzie Barge and Marineways Ltd.: founded 1930 — p. 14.
10.   Matsumoto Shipyards (founded 1949) — p. 14.
11.   The Lynnwood Inn, 1515 Barrow, North Vancouver: a Lowry drinking spot — p. 95.
12. ——— Dollarton Highway: built by relief crews in 1930 — p. 14.
13. = ■ ■ = Trans Canada Highway: connects Vancouver and North Vancouver. Until construction of the Second Narrows Bridge, automobile traffic used the railway bridge. The Lowrys would have travelled this bridge going between Dollarton and Vancouver.
14. · — — Keith Road: first road into the Dollarton/Deep Cove Area — p. 12.
    — · — Mount Seymour Parkway: originally Keith Road.
15. ······ Deep Cove Road
   ++++ Railway

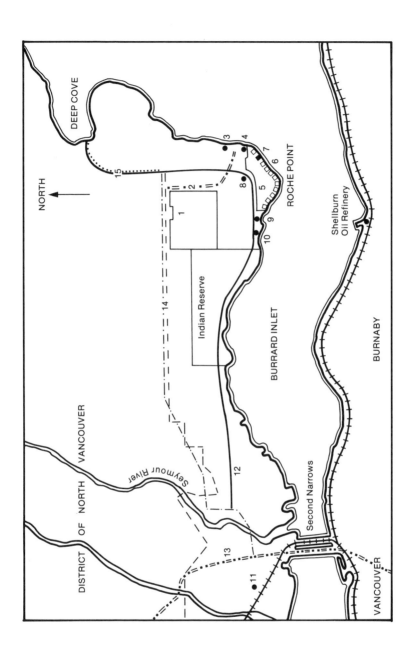

The locations of all sites on this map are approximate and it must be noted that the number of squatters' shacks fluctuated as did their owners or tenants; the foreshore has also changed over the years.

Note 1   Marjorie Kirk recalls rowing to Taylor Creek for water and adds that other squatters also went there from time to time. In "The Forest Path to the Spring" (237), Lowry describes "rowing to a spring about half a mile away, round the point with the lighthouse, and beyond the wharf of the barge company.... This stream ran all the year round but was so shallow you couldn't scoop your bucket into it."

Note 2   Mr. and Mrs. James Craige had two shacks side by side, and a small creek flowed near the boatshed.

Note 3   The Day shack belonged to Betty Day (Jimmy Craige's daughter) and her husband Douglas Day — it is a coincidence that another Douglas Day was one of the first Lowry biographers.

Note 4   B. & J. Craig: the shack belonging to Bill and Jean Craig (the son of Jimmy Craige and the sister of Downie Kirk).

Note 5   Levi/Maartman: Norman and Gloria Levi lived in this shack for a short time and then Ben Maartman, who owned the shack, moved in.

Note 6   It is not clear how many shacks away the Burts' shack was from the Lowrys'; they apparently moved into the Lowrys' shack after the Lowrys moved from the beach.

Note 7   Birney: Earle purchased his shack to hold a few parties but never lived on the beach and did not keep his shack long.

Note 8   Four Bells: According to Dollarton oldtimers, Mr. Bell was a railroad engineer from Edson, Alberta, who had a summer shack on the Dollarton beach; he had a wife and two children and a sign outside his shack read "Four Bells." The Bells are mentioned in some of the Lowrys' journals (p. 31) and in "The Forest Path to the Spring." In 1947 the Bells sold their shack to the Howick family. Mrs. Howick recalls that when they moved to the beach the Lowrys were friendly and came over to welcome them. Although Mrs. Howick did not get to know the

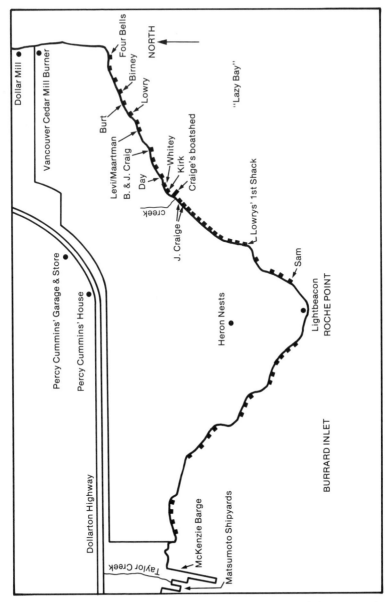

Lowrys well, her husband, Harry, an electrician, shared an interest in literature with Lowry.

Note 9   "Lazy Bay" was the name people in the village of Dollarton coined for the bay northeast of Roche Point.

This map shows the routes of the B.C. Coast Steamship Service (the official title for the C.P.R. Ferry Service) between Vancouver and Vancouver Island. In 1946 the Lowrys travelled from downtown Vancouver to Victoria. They then caught a bus to Nanaimo where they took a privately run ferry, the *Atrevida*, to Gabriola Island. They returned to Vancouver from Nanaimo via the C.P.R. Ferry.

It should be noted that a map of "Vancouver Bay" appears in Muriel Bradbrook's *Malcolm Lowry: His Art and Early Life* (86), but the ferry routes indicated are not those used by the C.P.R. Ferries in 1946. Map 4 is based on maps and other information found in Robert D. Turner's *The Pacific Princesses: an illustrated history of Canadian Pacific Railway's Princess fleet on the Pacific Northwest Coast* (Victoria, B.C.: Sono Nis Press, 1977).

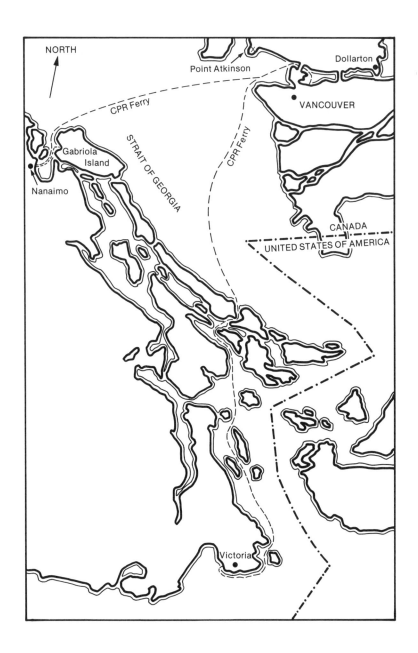

NORTH

Point Atkinson

Dollarton

CPR Ferry

VANCOUVER

Gabriola
Island

STRAIT OF GEORGIA

CPR Ferry

Nanaimo

CANADA

UNITED STATES OF AMERICA

Victoria

1. The old Nanaimo bus terminal, where the Lowrys arrived in 1946.
2. The Hotel Plaza (in 1985 the Villa Hotel), that Lowry refers to as the "Ocean Spray" in *October Ferry to Gabriola*.
3. The site of the restaurant owned by Alfred Mckee, the Esquire Coffee Shop, where the Lowrys had dinner before catching the ferry to Vancouver – p. 50.

Note 1: The ferry to Gabriola passed by Gallows Point and its lighthouse and Lowry used this site in *October Ferry*, calling it "Hangman's Point." According to Donald Graham, *Keepers of the Light: A History of British Columbia Lighthouses and Their Keepers* (1985), the point received its name after two native Indians were hung there for the murder of a shepherd in 1853.

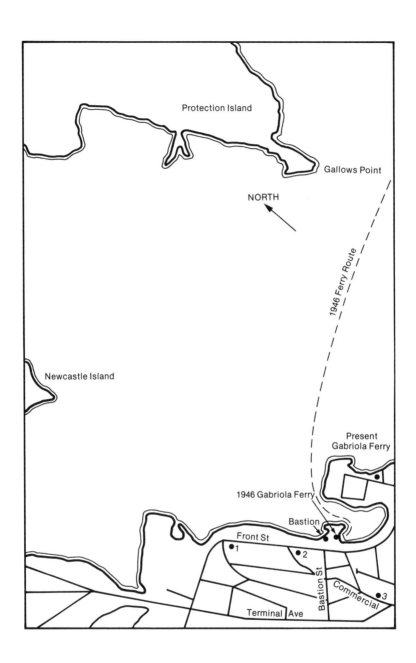

Protection Island

Gallows Point

NORTH

1946 Ferry Route

Newcastle Island

Present
Gabriola Ferry

1946 Gabriola Ferry

Bastion

Front St

●1

●2

Bastion St

Commercial

●3

Terminal Ave

KEY TO MAP 6 – GABRIOLA ISLAND 1946

1. Anderson Lodge (now the Surf Lodge), where the Lowrys stayed during their trip to Gabriola – p. 45 – 6.
2. Alfred and Angela McKee's cabin.
3. The bluff where the Lowrys and the McKees studied the night sky – p. 49.
4. Site of the Trenton Rest Home, which Lowry referred to as the Gabriola Convalescent Home in *October Ferry to Gabriola*.
5. The approximate site of the cabin that was offered to the Lowrys – p. 49.
6. The site of the Catholic Church. According to Alfred McKee the Lowrys did not travel to that end of the Island (p. 49), but they may have met the priest on the ferry, as indicated in *October Ferry to Gabriola*, Chapter 35 "The Perilous Chapel."

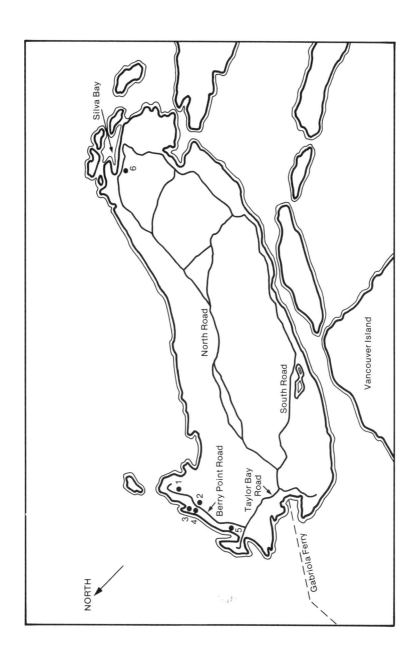

NORTH

Silva Bay

6

North Road

South Road

Vancouver Island

Berry Point Road

Taylor Bay Road

1
2
3
4
5

Gabriola Ferry

Appendix 2

HOLLYWOOD AND THE WAR
BY C. M. L.

Somewhere in Hollywood a soldier leaned against a radio. Round his head was a bloodstained bandage. In his muddy uniform he seemed rigid with listening. This man, an extra, despite his unlikelihood, was real. So was what he heard from Warsaw. His look, as of one who sees into hell but doesn't believe it, was real too.

Scene of the Exodus and the Retreat from Mons alike; the town where Charles Chaplin is making The Great Dictator, and where Mussolini's son had tried, unsuccessfully, in default of the Third Reich, to negotiate with Hal Roach, Hollywood the Unreal, where Marie Antoinette can see Juliet's tomb from the tumbril, and Waterloo and the Battle of the Somme are fought contiguously, had been jolted out of its timeless existence by the actuality of war.

How far a cry now were the headlines from the wisecracks of 1938! With a hey Nazi Nazi and a hot Ja Ja, they had laughed then. Now no one laughed. But everywhere one sensed a kind of fever as the circumscribed lives of the motion picture people narrowed down even further to a point of harrassed intensity and anxiety.

It was not only the recomputations, the adjustments of budgets, the distortion of schedules, or even the abandonment of pictures, caused by the cancellation of European contracts, with, inevitably, its threat of unemployment, which affected them: there was also the personal element. Joe E. Brown, making a farce, but unable to locate his eldest son in Europe. Ernest Lubisch, the director, with an infant daughter on the Athena; Annabella, with one in Paris. The English actors, and the French, David Niven, Charles Boyer, recalled to active service.

The broadcasting stations, N.B.C. and C.B.S., kept their loudspeakers going day and night with bulletins, news, speeches, eliminating or breaking into their normal programmes with an even more maddening regularity than their advertisements. Not that the latter had been completely discarded! Because, as someone pointed out, the Athenia might be taking one's relatives to the bottom of the ocean at one moment, while at the next, the familiar, gentlemanly words recommending this soup or that called one back, with agonizing complacency, to his immediate circle.

And all this, together with the static, the interference from foreign stations, the confusion of tongues, produced a pandemonium as indescribable as the advance of a mechanized army itself, so that finally one was forced to wonder whether or not our extra, or anyone else in Hollywood listening to the radio, was convinced that the war was real at all. Did it not seem, perhaps, on the contrary, an ultimate UNreality?

The subsequent confusion was self-extending to other Hollywood confusions, past and present.

One thought of Emil Jannings, that very German German, starred by Von Sternberg in "The Last Command," a picture about a great Russian general who ended as an extra in Hollywood; and of the violent Russian anti-Nazi film, "Dr. Mamlock," being shown downtown even while the Russo-German pact was coming into effect.

One thought of "Grand Illusion," showing elsewhere, that French film which won its director, Jules [sic] Renoir, the Legion of Honor, and which exhibited the essential camaraderie in a prison camp between the aristocracy of France and Germany during the last war, just as Pabst had exhibited in the German-made "Kameradschaft," a film once sponsored by the Duke of Windsor for a benefit performance for the unemployed in England, the fellowship between French and German miners during a disaster.

One thought, too, of Fritz Lang, the German director of "Metropolis," which presaged the Nazi regime, reduced to making 'quickies'; of Eisenstein, the Russian director, fired for making "The American Tragedy," and of Peter Lorre, whom Lang directed in his German film, "M," saying that Germany was too small for two monsters like Hitler and himself. Yet if Hollywood, as a touchstone of what is contradictory in America, and accustomed to take the unlikeliest in its stride, has been forced to accept this wildest of all contradictions as real, is it any wonder that a sense of nightmare, of something going on in another planet, a feeling that, in spite of experience, "We do not associate such dooms with ourselves," has crept into the national consciousness? Nevertheless, concerned with opposites, we must recognize that the converse is also true. A recent article in the American "Time," dealing with the period of delay just before we entered the war, contained these words: "Over the darkened cities that had become haunted and despairing islands, of the last nights together, of work never to be done, of children unseen, of dreams unfulfilled, over the countless acres of anguish, the ghosts of the last war and the ghosts of the next met to gain a moment longer." And in this magnificent passage it is difficult not to detect the whisper of a terrible "perhaps" to our friends, the American people themselves.

Reprinted from *The Daily Province*, Vancouver, 12 December 1939: 4.

THE REAL MR. CHIPS
BY MALCOLM LOWRY

Who is Mr. Chips?

If this question were included in one of the current and popular quizzes a multitude of people would answer, doubtless, that he was only the hero of the well-known novel and film, "Goodbye Mr. Chips." Or, possibly, they would say that he was a kind of symbolization of all beloved old schoolmasters, and in this assumption they might be equally correct. To myself he has always seemed a very living person indeed.

It is difficult, of course, to pin down the original of any character in fiction for few, even when drawn from life, escape wholly from belonging to the composite order of architecture. An attitude from this person, an idiosyncrasy from that, Smith's bowler hat, Jones' sea boots — such are the material which go to the creating of a character in a novel. In this respect Mr. Chips, like Sherlock Holmes or Stalky, is no exception. We may track him down to his lair in the real world but he will seem, in the flesh, both more and less than the character for which he was the point of departure.

Nevertheless, to me, he is always the Hooley and he was once the master of West House, The Leys, Cambridge.

Situated on the outskirts of the ancient university town, bounded by the fens on one side and Trumpington street on the other, The Leys, one of England's finer, if lesser known, public schools, has produced such novelists as James Hilton, such cricketers as F.R. Brown. The English school cricket team which was to have come to Canada this summer contained several Leysians, was captained by one.

It bears, however, little likeness to the Brookfield of the book or picture; actually this Brookfield, in the custom and usage of its scholars, far more nearly resembles Repton, a much older school, that actually put itself at the disposal of the film's director. What Leys and Brookfield have in common, besides the Hooley, is rather a matter of nomenclature, something which will also grant us an interesting sidelight on the mechanism of a novelist's mind.

On the far side of Trumpington street, opposite the Leys, is a brook; beyond that a street, Brookside, where our old East House used to be, and where, also, after he had retired, the Hooley lived. Hence, perhaps, since Leys means field, Brookfield! The Hooley was not only master of West when I was there some twelve years ago, but master of it twelve years before that, when my brother was there, and James Hilton was attracting some attention by his contributions to the Fortnightly, the school magazine under the Hooley's aegis. And it was Hooley, too, who encouraged Hilton with his first novel, Catherine Herself, published while he was still at the Leys, and which is now a collector's item.

The facts relating the Hooley to Mr. Chips either directly or by implication are too many to be accidental. Marriage is an exception, for he was always, to the best of my knowledge, single. But who, once having known the Hooley, could forget his habit of clearing his throat before opening? Or his meringues for tea?

His interest in games, too, and everything Leysian even after his retirement, his taking over the temporary headmastership, his difficulties as a young master — the Hooley was reported to have been mercilessly ragged, even to have fainted, at his first preparation — and his veneration by everybody as an old one, all these associations, in one way or another, have their counterparts in the novel.

Yet there is an irreducible logic about coincidences which sometimes justifies them in their own right. For instance, at about the time of the Hooley's retirement, a young, unknown Shakesperean actor was beginning to make his mark in a struggling repertory company at the Festival Theatre in Newmarket Road, Cambridge, not 10 minutes walk from Brookside.

Although there is indeed nothing to show that Robert Donat, for it was he, ever met the Hooley, or has since associated in any way his performance as Mr. Chips with the Leys or his sojourn at Cambridge, the fact remains that on his way to the theatre he must very frequently have passed not only the school but the Hooley's new home, and it is not difficult to imagine the actor standing beside the original of the character that was to bring him his greatest acclaim, among the knot of visitors attracted to a school match.

As a matter of fact, the Hooley was something of an actor himself. Nobody in the west dormitories who was lucky enough to hear him read Erckmann-Chatrian's The Bells, taking all the parts and even supplying the effects with a pencil and biscuit tin, will ever forget it: not Henry Irving with his whole company could have exceeded his one man show in dramatic intensity.

Since the Hooley may have been embarrassed, in spite of any pride in the achievement of his pupil, by a book whose widespread popularity its author could scarcely have foreseen, I think it as well to state here he never was and never could be the doddering, absent-minded old man of the picture, however sympathetically portrayed. Up to a few years ago the Hooley was a crack fives player, an energetic tennis player, a vigorous walker. He had a brilliant incisive wit. And there is no reason to suppose that he does not possess all these capabilities today.

He possessed an excellent memory and I wonder if he recalls publishing, about 1916, in the Fortnightly, a verse of James Hilton's beginning:

"If, by 1941
When we have got the hated Hun
And he, at least, can no more stun
Our senses with a hidden gun . . ."

The rest of the drollery escapes me, but let us hope, as the new year approaches, that it ended in as comfortably prophetic a manner as it began.

Reprinted from *The Daily Province*, Vancouver, 13 December 1939: 4.

WHERE DID THAT ONE GO TO,'ERBERT?

(A.P.H., author of the lampoon, "Where is Lance?" reprinted from London's Punch in a recent Daily Province, is A.P. Herbert, also author of "The Water Gipsies," "Holy Deadlock," etc., and a member of Parliament, which institution has itself been shaken by his emancipatory opinions.)

So what, if Lance the Leftist, did shout once for "Arms for Spain"?
For other valid reasons, so did J.B.S. Haldane.
And so did Mann and Hemingway, good democrats and true,
And many others I could mention: even, perhaps you.
Come, come, weren't you a "rebel" A.P.H., despite your looks,

146

And all the beer and skittles of your admirable books?
You've had radical moments, sir: admit it, they weren't warm,
Those agitations were red-hot, for marital reform!
And if Russians seemed to Steve a mystical solution
He's not the only one two-timed by "Comes the Revolution."
Weren't you yourself quite startled, since this latest war began,
To discover that the vaunted Bear can't even *walk* like Man?
Modern Mervyn may be mawkish, and Ermyntrude a tramp,
But since we do not put them in a concentration camp.
And since the fight's for freedom, and since, after the war,
With brains blown out they may behave exactly as before,
Why not tell our Know-all Nesta now, our poor old Percy Pink,
The fact that this fight's for the right to say just what they think?
Else when Stalin dines on daschunds, and Molotov on Hess,
And Goebbles gobbles rush funds intended for the mess,
When vodka is verboten, when sauerkraut's but a dream,
And the last iron cross is eaten and there's shrapnel in the cream,
All the parlor Bolsheviki will be pinking once again.
(Still, where would be the Empire if we'd no one to complain?)
But apart from that it's boring, they ought to have the tip
There's really no objection to their indoor Marxmanship.
And now each man's a Left and Right within him, as it were,
And age may swing the coalition just as well as war,
When all of us must emulate, each fellow in his way,
The celebrated Vicar lately domiciled at Bray.
Now Left is Right and Right is Left ever the twain shall meet,
And your lampoon which raps the Left might be a right defeat —
A worthier target for your wit! The more especially,
Since Lance has upped and ruddy joined the bleeding infantry.

                         — Malcolm Lowry

Reprinted from *The Daily Province*, Vancouver, 29 December
1939:4.

Appendix 3

HAPPINESS

Blue mountains with snow and blue cold rough water,
A wild sky full of stars at rising
And Venus and the gibbous moon at sunrise,
Gulls following a motorboat against the wind,
Trees with branches rooted in air—
Sitting in the sun at noon with the furiously
Smoking shadow of the shack chimney—
Eagles drive downward in one,
Terns blow backward,
A new kind of tobacco at eleven,
And my love returning on the four o'clock bus
— My God, why have you given this to us?

(From *Selected Poems of Malcolm Lowry*, 53.)

SESTINA IN A CANTINA

Scene: A waterfront tavern in Vera Cruz at daybreak.

LEGION

Watching this dawn's mnemonic of old dawning:
Jonquil-colored, delicate, some in prison,
Green dawns of drinking tenderer than sunset,
But clean and delicate like dawns of ocean
Flooding the heart with pale light in which the horrors
Stampede like plump wolves in distorting mirrors.

Oh, we have seen ourselves in many mirrors;
Confusing all our sunsets with the dawning,
Investing every tongue and leaf with horrors,
And every stranger overtones for prison,
And seeing mainly in the nauseous ocean
The last shot of our life before the sunset.

ST. LUKE (a ship's doctor)

How long since you have really seen a sunset?
The mind has many slanting lying mirrors,
The mind is like that sparkling greenhouse ocean
Glass-deceptive in the Bengal dawning:
The mind has ways of keeping us in prison,
The better there to supervise its horrors.

SIR PHILIP SIDNEY

Why do you not, sir, organize your horrors
And shoot them one day, preferably at sunset,
That we may wake up next day not in prison,
No more deceived by lies and many mirrors,
And go down to the cold beach at dawning
To lave away the past in colder ocean?

ST. LUKE

No longer is there freedom on the ocean.
And even if there were, he likes his horrors,
And if he shot them would do so at dawning
That he might have acquired some more by sunset,
Breaking them in by that time before mirrors
To thoughts of spending many nights in prison.

LEGION

The fungus-colored sky of dawns in prison,
The fate that broods on every pictured ocean,
The fatal conversations before mirrors,
The fiends and all the spindly breeds of horrors,
Have shattered by their beauty every sunset
And rendered quite intolerable old dawning.

The oxen standing motionless at dawning —
Outside our tavern now, outside our prison —
Red through the wagon wheels, jalousies like sunset,
Swinging now in a sky as calm as ocean,
Where Venus hangs her obscene horn of horrors
For us now swaying in a hall of mirrors —

Such horrid beauty maddened all my mirrors,
Has burst in heart's eye sanity of dawning,
No chamber in my house brimful of horrors
But does not whisper of some dreadful prison,
Worse than all ships dithering through the ocean
Tottering like drunkards, arms upraised at sunset.

RICHARD III (a barman)

Vain derelict all avid for the sunset!
Shine out fair sun till you have brought new mirrors
That you may see your shadow pass the ocean,
And sunken no more pass our way at dawning,
But lie on the cold stone sea floor of some prison,
A chunk of sodden driftwood gnawed by horrors.

LEGION

At first I never looked on them as horrors;
But one day I was drinking hard near sunset,
And suddenly saw the world as a giant prison,
Ruled by tossing moose-heads, with hand mirrors,
And heard the voice of the idiot speak at dawning,
And since that time have dwelt beside the ocean.

EL UNIVERSAL (early edition)

Did no one speak of love beside the ocean,
Have you not felt, even among your horrors,
Granting them, there was such a thing as dawning,
A dawning for man whose star seems now at sunset,
Like million-sheeted scarlet dusty mirrors,
But one day must be led out of his prison?

LEGION

I see myself as all mankind in prison,
With hands outstretched to lanterns by the ocean;
i see myself as all mankind in mirrors,
Babbling of love while at his back rise horrors
Ready to suck the blood out of the sunset
And amputate the godhead of the dawning.

THE SWINE

And now the dawning drives us from our prison
Into the dawn like sunset, into the ocean,
Bereaving him of horrors, but leaving him his mirrors. . . .

(From *Selected Poems of Malcolm Lowry*, 41 – 44.)

Appendix 4

The following story written by William McConnell is based on a visit with Lowry in Dollarton. It first appeared in the *Malcolm Lowry Review*, Numbers 17 & 18, Fall 1985 & Spring 1986; since that time it has been revised.

IN SEARCH OF THE WORD

When Grant arrived at the waterfront shack it was deserted. True, the door wasn't locked, for Clement seldom locked anything except outward show of his emotions.

Standing in the hot July sun which was baking the splintery planks of the platform on which the shack perched slightly above high-tide mark, Grant sniffed the quiet oldness emanating from the cedar shakes which framed the windows. In a few moments he grew restive feeling that after the phone call of the night before there should have been at least a spiral of smoke rising from the tin chimney. Or Clement could have left a note, a few embers burning in his clay repaired stove, the door ajar — some slight sign that the invitation was not meaningless, another cypher in their long coded relationship. He nervously patted the fat wad of manuscript in his pocket. Their meetings were so seldom he invariably brought some of his own writing to read. Odd, Clement thought every writer, apart from himself, a genius.

Grant set down the packsack, careful that the gallon of wine didn't bump the deck too hard. Perhaps Clement had meant they spend Sunday afternoon rather than Saturday together. His messages were always so cryptic as if he didn't trust the other with all information.

Grant laughed, wondering if he should look for a forked stick with a white tucked message on it reading,

> Now proceed three hundred foot paces to the North. Sight between Cypress Tree on the middle cliff of the varicosed ridge, then turn right...

Grant actually looked about in the underbrush which rose sheer behind him on the shore of the inlet for some omen which might supplement Clement's message. It only need to read,

> Three o'clock, about. Make it three o'clock...

For the time had not been mentioned and afternoons stretch like elastic bands if one is waiting in the sun, tired from all night spent in the Emergency Ward where he was interning.

The Salal and serrated Oregon Grape leaves winked back at him, reflecting the sunlight dappled up from the saltchuck, as if saying, "Now take it easy, there's a message somewhere about; just guess, you only need guess where and how. There will be a word somewhere. One can't make it too easy, you know." And higher than the thick undergrowth the Cedars and Second-growth Firs appeared to nod gently in agreement, secretly amused he suspected but too dignified to show it.

Grant reflected that he could settle down in the shade of the adjacent woodshed and read one of the books he had bought for Clement. (Clement never purchased books, always borrowed them from friends or library, for a book without an owner could hardly be criticised; it was the ownership actually he pilloried, and a book without an owner was to him insensate.)

Or, for that matter, he, Grant, could violate the closed door, swing it simply on its hinges and walk in. Perhaps Clement was asleep and hadn't heard his halloo.

He hallooed a second time; it brought the same response — a warping cry from two Seagulls perched on driftwood motionless on the low-tide mark fifty feet out from the ochre and green barnacled rocks. He was about to repeat his hail when the chugging of a beachcomber's gas boat dissuaded him. He knew nothing of Clement's relationship with his fishermen neighbours, save what was revealed in Clement's published stories and this, while it could never be false, might be such he could expect a rifle-shot, a fusilade of rocks or even a mysterious fireball thrown in his direction by a malignant source.

Just as Grant was about to climb down the ladder to the beach shingle he heard a slithering descent down the trail which led from the cliff to the cabin.

Clement's cadaverous disjointed body jacknifed onto the planking with a cheery wave ('much like the striking of a flag by an overjoyed surrendering soldier,' Grant thought).

"Hello Clement."

They stood, after moving closer to the edge of the piling which marked squatters rights. Clement, shy after his first effusion, waved and mumbled, "Tide's out" as if apologising for the moon, the seasons and, most importantly, his absence at Grant's arrival.

Grant understood the guised apology. His spirits rose. The two seagulls skorked again when they heard the voices, at which

Clement allowed his mouth to spread and slightly open before saying with pride:

"Mutt and Jeff. I feed them. Not symbolic characters for a change, Grant. Just Mutt and Jeff. The only glaucous-winged gulls on the Inlet with a talent for conversation—vulgar conversation, mind. Gossip, bitching about the tide, lack of scraps, thieving crows, not enough females. One of my neighbours (here he glanced darkly to the right, as if expecting an ambuscade) hates Mutt and Jeff. Shot at 'em once. His trigger finger will turn to stone."

And at Grant's now comfortable silence, "But how are you? Com'in, com'in!"

They entered the two room shack just as the tide started to change with seven identically sized rollers cresting in. These upset Mutt and Jeff who slipped into the water and bobbed away from the beach.

"Tide's changed," Clement remarked irrelevantly while he fussed by shaking oilclothed table free of crumbs. "Yes, how are you?"

"Brought you books and, for us, some wine," Grant replied while he disgorged the backpack, embarrassed with the process. Now he was the shy one, shy as he knew Clement was making too much of an initial effort, anxious that he wouldn't later subside into self-torturing grunts when talk for both would be so important.

"Cheap wine—white, but it's a gallon."

"Ah, I'll rinse some glasses and we'll have an anticipatory drink."

In ten minutes they settled down to sip during which they completed the small talk on which survival depended.

"Writing?" Grant tentatively jabbed at Clement, whose mid-west flattened voice took on eagerness when he replied.

"Yes. No. Two weeks now. Like rolling a cigarette but making it too tight to draw. It's not loose enough. It's discoloured about its edges, patchy, not fresh and smooth. The novel. I started at the end to get some balance. Didn't get balance, it teetered with too much climactic weight. So I started in the middle and re-wrote what I read to you last time you were here. Didn't work. Seems tangled up with climaxes before the end of each chapter. If it weren't so bad I'd snipsnip it apart and make short stories of it and sell them to Radio. Perhaps that's why I'm writing that way, do you think?" And his blue left eye raised seemed to mutely seek guidance.

Grant avoided these appeals for professional opinion. Unlike Clement, he was the amateur. Too, his medical training had induced elaborate caution in diagnosis, caution which he, when writing, constantly inhibited. Not he to start at the end or the middle.

154

"And you?" Clement enquired kindly. "Finish that story? The one about yourself. Been thinking, thinking about that, y'know. Needs one word, one word to set its tone. Been searching for the word. Thinking about it when I fell off the rock. Imagine that! Searching for a word and fall off a rock just as if I were searching for an exact cedar plank for the dock. You knew I fell, of course?"

Grant nodded. They filled their glasses again while excess moisture collected in their armpits. Clement rose and opened the windows facing the water.

"Yes I fell. Fell, mind you, when looking for the exact word. Never fallen since I was a child and then no boulders to fall from, only wet or dusty ground. I think that's why I love this place so much. Every conceivable kind of rock if you look for it. What better way to find the exact word than to prowl at low tide and examine each rock, to find the one which fits the word you need. Rocks are a key to words. They unlock the secret of any phrase. Have I told you that before?"

This time their glasses were emptied faster and, when again filled, a slight slopping occurred.

Grant sniffed his glass before speaking, "I knew, yet I didn't know. Sensed it, I suppose. Something like that." He was always inarticulate when this range of communication was attained. Work in Pathology in his final year, he suspected. Grant knew Clement sensed his block and was not troubled by it. Grant went on:

"Some damage, I suppose. Your back is probably out of kilter. You'll be running into some Chiropractor for treatment if it persists."

Clement stared at him with a trace of indignation. "I looked for you, Grant. Yelled to the bastards at the hospital, 'Where's Doc Grant? Hold on you sons of bitches. Don't dare touch me with a knife till Doc Grant's been consulted. Where the hell is he?' "

Grant squirmed. He couldn't seem to make his friend realise that he was only an interne, that he had no status except to bandage, deliver the odd baby when the regular doctor was late, take off casts and dabble under supervision in the Emergency Ward. He knew that to Clement, because he had studied for eight years and was called a doctor, he was a doctor. Reality was dispelled by alchemy.

"What hospital?" Grant enquired.

But Clement didn't hear him, so intent was he on the core of the matter. He settled down on his chair after filling their glasses again, picked his coal-black cat up to his lap and stroked her.

"You see," Clement went on, his eyes now downcast to the cat, "the awful thing was they didn't know you, had never heard of you. How could that be?"

Grant clutched the side of his rattan chair at the inscrutable disbelief in his friend's voice. Yes, that he wasn't known, that in itself was a betrayal.

"I tried to explain how it happened. You see, these people had faces which were all alike, oval shaped. Remember those drawings, the charcoal ones, we saw in the gallery in San Francisco? Remember how you remarked to me, 'Clement,' you said, 'the emptiness is the key. Look closer and don't be blind. All the faces appear to be different. But look closely you'll see they are the same.' Well, that's the way it was with all these people who crowded around my bed. They had oval faces which appeared to be quite different until you examined each one carefully, to really look closer as you had enjoined me in San Francisco. They were all alike in their emptiness. That's what was so frightening."

He deposited the cat on the floor gently and paced up and down the sloping floor. "That and the cowls. Some of them were cowled. It made their faces even more oval shaped and empty."

Grant realised he had been taken to the Catholic hospital though he didn't enlighten him for he knew Clement had never been in a hospital before. Perhaps this was why he had no comprehension of Grant's routine. It was amazing that one who had been in so many odd corners of the world knew so little about its institutions. Amazing, that is, until one remembered the sifting quality his mind possessed, the same quality which made his writing so powerful and insistent.

Clement stopped pacing and stared out at the blue water. "But wait. The tide's just right. I have some lumber I salvaged yesterday. Would you mind rowing around the Point with me? It won't take long."

And, as he rowed with powerful choppy strokes, "I want to extend my wharf so I can pace it when blocked in my writing. It's thirty-four paces now and I feel fifty should be adequate."

For the next half hour they brought the beachcombed lumber back and piled it beyond the reach of high tide, talking the while of what they had written and done during the previous months.

On this ground Grant was more voluble while Clement shyer. Grant explained how he had encountered a block in his writing and hadn't cleared it no matter what he tried. He explained it was a matter of will if one is allowed the time. But he was on twelve hour shifts so perhaps it was a question of energy.

When they re-entered the shack they fried cod fillets from a fish which had been left on the dock during their final trip.

"Some fisherman," Clement chuckled. "Which one is unimportant except that I'll have to nod to each one for fear of missing the donor. Perhaps it's the one who stole my fender log during the last storm; he's doing penance in his own way. Don't you think a beautiful Ling cod is magnificent penance? Getting a fisherman to part with a fish is like getting a writer to slice out a chapter. One of the Pot fishermen left a crab one day. I tried to eat it raw I knew so little about them. Yet, the fisherman and I know the sea thoroughly, each in our own way."

Grant, who had read one of Clement's short stories about the Gulf of Mexico, readily nodded in agreement.

Eating completed they took their dishes outside and scoured them in the sand below the shack before settling down again with cigarettes and wine. Imperceptibly afternoon had become evening and a rising breeze blowing through the windows brought chill so Clement lit the stove and partially closed the windows. A tanker across the Bay hooted as it slipped away from the refinery.

Grant was anxious to read what he had brought but Clement didn't give him an opening. He was still obsessed with the aftermath of his accident.

"You see, Grant, the whole point of the matter was we were both searching for the exact word. I knew that in the second I fell from the rock. That's the only thing which made the fall have resolve and meaning. I tried to explain that to them but all they did was send in a funny little Doctor who wanted to chat about my childhood. He wasn't the one who fixed my leg, of course. Him I saw quite often in the Hospital where I thought quite highly of him, the Surgeon, a Specialist."

The tanker hooted again and Clement crossed to the window and looked out. "That's the Shell Princess. She takes bunker oil to San Francisco. I sailed on a tanker years ago. To the Far East."

Turning back, he continued. "Revised my opinion when I went to his Surgery for a check-up."

"The Surgeon?"

"Yes, comfortably fed fellow. Huge office. Had to go once a week for a month. His place was disconcerting – the office was designed to wait in but after you got into his Surgery it seemed as if you had left something of yourself behind. Do people have that feeling in your office? No, that's right, I remember you telling me you had no office yet.

"In the hospital he seemed a sincere fellow with a good sense of humour. But that was before the Day of the Leg."

He paused to refill his glass unsteadily, not from the wine but the recollection.

"Reminded me of a fellow I met on the beach in San Diego. Tanned and fit, muscles in shape, but inside he was twisted. His inside didn't belong to his outside. Anyway, it was the Day of the Leg which, to use a horribly appropriate word, severed our relationship of Doctor-Patient.

"We had become quite chummy. In the hospital he didn't seem to think it was odd that I fell looking for the exact word. He made some quite sensible remarks about Faulkner's work. But on this visit he remarked that for a while he'd thought he might have to amputate the leg but it mended quite nicely. He must have sensed the horror with which I received this remark. But did it affect him?

"No Grant. Know what he did. He waved to a cabinet behind me. Shades of Caligari! He traced a leg with his hands, complete from hip to heel, just as if he were describing the shape of Italy and with the same impersonality. When I finally screwed up the courage to turn and look at the glass cabinet, what do you think it contained, Grant?"

The question was rhetorical for Clement was sweating now and his eyes were dilated.

"Limbs, Grant! Pink and white artificial limbs. And he said, quite calmly, that they worked almost as well as real ones. This was the man to whom I told of our search for the word! God, how you can be fooled by people — how they can trick and deceive you!"

Clement paced the floor again.

"Pink and white. Smooth as alabaster, as if they had been severed from drowned choir girls then varnished with preservative. I only had glanced at them, mind, but their obscene freshness was so great I expected them to descend at his signal and march across his Surgery towards me.

"To think I was nearly taken in by this fellow. When he had traced the Italy he had done so with a smile, a fondness. Needless to say I scrambled out of there and never went back. How could you trust yourself to a person like that Grant? Why don't you Doctors drum out fellows like that?

"You understand don't you, Grant? It's not often I've failed you, friend, but this time you'll have to struggle alone. You understand that I would never be able to find the right word we wanted, the exact shading we had discussed and agreed upon. Every time I laboured for it that man's haunted me as he described his beautiful limbs, each neatly severed from some ghastly source to be grafted onto a living trunk."

His agony was so great it threatened momentarily to spill over into tears and both knew their friendship would be unable to survive such a display. Hurriedly they rose, filled their glasses, drained them with a mutual smile making Grant's leave-taking brisk, almost curt.

Outside, climbing the path, Grant hurried more than his condition really allowed. He must reach the top. There would be light and the soon-arriving bus. He knew that while his friend thought he had failed him in not discovering the exact word (which would never have fitted in any event, for words are too ephemeral to be taken captive) he had given him something more vital, the will to write again.

Notes

NOTES TO THE INTRODUCTION

1. Malcolm Lowry, "Through the Panama," *Hear us O Lord from heaven thy dwelling place* (Philadelphia and New York: J.B. Lippincott, 1961), 31.

2. *Selected Letters Of Malcolm Lowry*, edited by Harvey Breit & Margerie Bonner Lowry (Philadelphia and New York: J.B. Lippincott, 1965), 338 – 339. All subsequent references will appear parenthetically in the body of the text.

3. Dr. C.G. McNeill had a practice in Deep Cove, near Dollarton. His recollections, "Malcolm Lowry Visits the Doctor," have been published in *American Review* 17 (Spring, 1973): 35 – 39, and in *Malcolm Lowry: Psalms and Songs*, edited by Margerie Lowry (New York: New American Library, 1975).

4. For a complete reading of "After publication of *Under the Volcano*," see *Selected Poems of Malcolm Lowry*, edited by Earle Birney (San Francisco: City Lights Books, 1962), 78.

5. Douglas Day, *Malcolm Lowry: A Biography* (New York: Oxford University Press, 1973); M.C. Bradbrook, *Malcolm Lowry: His Art and Early Life* (London: Cambridge University Press, 1974); Gordon Bowker, *Malcolm Lowry Remembered* (London: Ariel Books, 1985). Day provides general information and examines Lowry's life using a Freudian approach; Bradbrook examines and clarifies details of Lowry's early years and his student days at Cambridge; through a collection of reminiscences, particularly an interview with Lowry's first wife (Jan Gabrial), Bowker further clarifies events of Lowry's life and provides insights into Lowry's life and personality.

NOTES TO CHAPTER ONE

1. From an interview with Russell Lowry (Malcolm's brother) in Bowker's *Malcolm Lowry Remembered*, 18.

2. Russell Lowry in Bowker's *Malcolm Lowry Remembered*, 18.

3. Bradbrook, *Malcolm Lowry: His Art and Early Life*, 25. Bradbrook also states that Evelyn Lowry suffered menopausal problems in Lowry's childhood, thereby increasing her absences from the family. As a result Lowry suffered from maternal deprivation (Bradbrook, 25 – 26).

4. Day, *Malcolm Lowry*, 74.

5. This woman, who now resides in Vancouver, British Columbia, wishes to remain anonymous. To date no other recollections from the Lowry family's neighbours in England have been published. Other individuals wishing to remain anonymous will not be specified in the text.

6. Russell Lowry, "Preface: Malcolm—A Closer Look," in *The Art of Malcolm Lowry*, edited by Anne Smith (London: Vision Press, 1978), p. 12. In the Preface to this book (9–27), and in Bowker's *Malcolm Lowry Remembered* (17–22), Russell Lowry discusses his brother's boyhood and adolescence, adding to and refuting some of Lowry's descriptions of his youth.

7. Bradbrook, *Malcolm Lowry: His Art and Early Life*, 110.

8. "An Autopsy On This Childhood Then Reveals" (Box 4, Folder 15) University of British Columbia Library, Special Collections Division. All subsequent references to materials held in the Special Collections Division of the University of B.C. will appear in the body of the text, parenthetically, as: (U.B.C., with box and folder number).

9. Russell Lowry, from the Preface of Smith's *The Art of Malcolm Lowry*, 25.

10. Day, *Malcolm Lowry*, 78. A more general discussion of Lowry's activities at the Leys are to be found in Day, 78–90.

11. Photocopies of Lowry's hockey reports, as well as his prose and verse writings for *The Fortnightly*, are to be found in Box 33 of "The Malcolm Lowry Collection," Special Collections, U.B.C.

12. From an interview with Russell Lowry in Bowker's *Malcolm Lowry Remembered*, 19–20.

13. Day, *Malcolm Lowry*, 88–90; an interview with Ronnie Hill in Bowker's *Malcolm Lowry Remembered*, 22–26.

14. *The London Evening News* 14 May 1927: 5.

15. A letter from Joseph Ward, one of Lowry's shipmates on the *Pyrrhus*, relates some of the crew's attitudes as well as some of Lowry's experiences on the freighter: to be found in Bowker's *Malcolm Lowry Remembered*, 33–34.

16. In Smith's *The Art of Malcolm Lowry*, 21, Russell Lowry remembers that Malcolm was home in England for most of the summer of 1930 and therefore could not have worked on a Norwegian freighter. In *Malcolm Lowry: A Biography*, 121–122, Day outlines some of Lowry's

differing versions of his trip to Norway, as recalled by Margerie Lowry and James Stern.

17. This information is taken from Michael Mercer's play *Goodnight Disgrace*, a co-production with Shakespeare Plus, as performed with Graeme Campbell and Ron Hadler, at The Vancouver Playhouse, September 1985; as published in *Canadian Theatre Review* 41 (Winter 1984): 73 – 131; and from a lecture given by Michael Mercer in "A Canadian Play in Context Series," sponsored by the University of British Columbia, 1985.

18. Conrad Aiken, "Malcolm Lowry: A Note," *Canadian Literature* 8 (Spring, 1961): 30.

19. According to Day, Lowry's new friends included Michael Redgrave, Wynyard Browne, William Empson, Hugh Sykes-Davies, Kathleen Raine, Douglas Cooper, Gerald Noxon, John Davenport, and Arthur Calder-Marshall. Many of these friends from the 1930s have published their recollections of Lowry; a number are to be found in Bowker's *Malcolm Lowry Remembered*. Lowry is also known to have been the model for the character James Dowd in Charlotte Haldane's *I Bring Not Peace*, a novel she dedicated to Lowry.

20. From the Preface to Smith's *The Art of Malcolm Lowry*, 20 – 23.

21. Aiken, "Malcolm Lowry: A Note," 30.

22. According to Bradbrook, *Malcolm Lowry: His Art and Early Life* (113 – 114, 116, 161 – 162), Lowry testified at the inquest but did not tell his parents of this occurrence. The version of Fitte's suicide as told to Margerie is to be found in Day, *Malcolm Lowry*, 138 – 139. For a discussion of Wensleydale, who appears in drafts of *Dark as the Grave Wherein my Friend is Laid*, the unpublished drafts of *The Ordeal of Sigbjorn Wilderness*, and the few surviving pages of *In Ballast to the White Sea*, see Day, 139, 142 – 144.

23. From an interview with Ian Parsons in Bowker's *Malcolm Lowry Remembered*, 80 – 82.

24. From Robert Duncan's (Robert Duncan Productions Ltd., Montreal) 1975 interview with Jan Gabrial (Lowry's first wife), as published in Bowker's *Malcolm Lowry Remembered*, 94.

25. For more information on Lowry in New York in 1935 – 1936 see the interview with Eric Estoric, 103 – 106, and the interview with Jan Gabrial, 91 – 102, in Bowker's *Malcolm Lowry Remembered*.

26. From Robert Duncan's 1975 interview with Jan Gabrial as published in Bowker's *Malcolm Lowry Remembered*, 122.

27. In *Malcolm Lowry: A Biography*, 252 – 253, Day states that both Arthur Lowry and Parks probably wanted to ensure that Malcolm would not be involved in the divorce proceedings; the move would also ensure that Malcolm and Jan would not reconcile.

NOTES TO CHAPTER TWO

1. Malcolm Lowry, *Under the Volcano* (Philadelphia and New York: J.B. Lippincott Company, 1965), 121.

2. Malcolm Lowry, "The Bravest Boat," *Hear us O Lord*, 17.

3. Lowry, *Under the Volcano*, 121.

4. "Hollywood And The War" and "The Real Mr. Chips" were reprinted in the *Malcolm Lowry Newsletter* 11 (Fall, 1982): 4 – 10 (now *The Malcolm Lowry Review*). Comments about these articles were made by Paul Tiessen in the *Malcolm Lowry Newsletter* 10 (Spring, 1982): 11 – 13. For a general discussion of Lowry's use of cinematic techinques see Paul Tiessen's article "Malcolm Lowry and the Cinema," *Canadian Literature* 44 (Spring, 1970): 38 – 49; also published in *Malcolm Lowry: The Man And His Work* edited by George Woodcock (Vancouver: University of British Columbia Press, 1971), 133 – 143.

5. Sherrill Grace, *The Voyage That Never Ends: Malcolm Lowry's Fiction* (Vancouver: University of British Columbia Press, 1982), 38.

6. Malcolm Lowry, *October Ferry to Gabriola* (New York: The World Publishing Company, 1970), 197.

7. G.W. Taylor, *Timber: History of the Forest Industry in B.C.* (Vancouver: J.J. Douglas Ltd., 1975), 100.

8. Robert Dollar, *Memoirs of Robert Dollar* Vol. II. (San Francisco: W.S. Van Cott & Co., 1921), 13.

9. According to the report "Subdivision Planned For Dollarton Site," *The Vancouver Sun* 17 May 1944: 1, the Dollar Mill was sold to the Northwest Bay Logging Company, an H.R. MacMillan (later known as Macmillan Bloedel Ltd.) subsidiary located on Vancouver Island.

10. Kathleen Marjorie Woodward-Reynolds, "A History of the City and District of North Vancouver" (Master's Thesis, University of British Columbia, 1943), 135.

11.   In "Eridanus: Another View," published in *The Malcolm Lowry Review* 17 & 18 (Fall 1985 & Spring 1986), Sheryl Salloum noted that McKenzie Derrick was established in 1935. From further discussions with the owner, Bob Mckenzie, it is now known that the company began operations in the Dollarton area in 1930.

12.   Noram Group of Consulting Companies Ltd., *The First Fifty Years: Shellburn 1932 – 1982* (Vancouver: Shell Canada Limited, 1982), 12 – 21.

13.   Lowry, *October Ferry to Gabriola*, 157.

14.   Bradbrook, *Malcolm Lowry: His Art and Early Life*, 1.

15.   Lowry, "The Forest Path to the Spring," *Hear us O Lord*, 221.

16.   Interview with Marjorie Kirk, March 1985.

17.   Day, *Malcolm Lowry*, 277 – 278.

18.   Day, *Malcolm Lowry*, 288.

19.   Malcolm Lowry, *Dark as the Grave Wherein my Friend is Laid* (Toronto: General Publishing Company, Ltd., 1968), 90.

20.   An example of a "Margie version" is in the MS of *Dark as the Grave Wherein my Friend is Laid*, (U.B.C. 8:20).

21.   In her article "Margerie Bonner's Three Forgotten Novels," *Journal of Modern Literature* 6, 2 (April 1977): 321 – 324, Sherrill Grace discusses Margerie Lowry's contribution to her husband's life and works.

22.   The Lowrys' screenplay is unpublished and is held at the Special Collections Library at the University of B.C.; the Lowrys' notes to the screenplay have been published by Bruccoli Clark, *Notes on a Screenplay for F. Scott Fitzgerald's "Tender Is the Night"* (1976).

23.   For discussions of the influence of Stansfeld-Jones and the Cabbala in Lowry's works see Perle Epstein's *The Private Labyrinth of Malcolm Lowry: Under the Volcano and the Cabbala*, and Tony Kilgallin's *Lowry*.

24.   Initially the Lowrys were on friendly terms with Cummins but over the years the relationship became strained. According to Dollarton old-timers, Cummins was often upset because the Lowrys' grocery bills were outstanding for long periods. Lowry complained that after the fire Cummins gave them banana sandwiches, and in numerous letters Lowry

expressed frustration with Cummins' efficiency as a postmaster, blaming Cummins for delayed or wayward mail.

25. Noxon's first visit to Dollarton appears to have been in 1942. At that time the Lowrys did not have any literary acquaintances in Vancouver.

26. According to Paul Tiessen, the Lowrys moved from Oakville to Niagara-on-the-Lake in October 1944. Note 9 of *The Malcolm Lowry Review* 17 & 18 (Fall 1985 & Spring 1986): 24.

27. A complete transcription of Gerald Noxon's rehearsal tape, with introductory comments by Paul Tiessen, can be found in *The Malcolm Lowry Review* 17 & 18 (Fall 1985 & Spring 1986): 10 – 24.

28. *Roslyn Park Sub-Division*, sales brochure of John R. Sigmore Limited (Sept. 1944), North Shore Museum and Archives, North Vancouver, British Columbia, Canada: #85 – 11.

29. Malcolm Lowry, "Gin and Goldenrod," *Hear us O Lord*, 203 – 204.

30. Bill Ryan, "Filthy Waterfront Hovels Doomed by New Civic Edict," *The Vancouver Sun* 22 March 1950: 21.

31. Anonymous information from the parents of one of the boys.

32. Lowry, "The Forest Path to the Spring," *Hear us O Lord*, 235 – 236.

33. See *Selected Letters*, 118.

34. Malcolm Lowry, "Present Estate of Pompeii," *Hear us O Lord*, 180.

35. From Margerie Lowry's book review of *Notes From the Century Before: A Journal From British Columbia*, by Edward Hoaglund; see also the Margerie Lowry Papers, University of B.C. (51:31).

36. "Town Planners Approve Roche Point Park," *North Arm News*, 15 Sept. 1949: 1. North Shore Museum and Archives: #85 – 11.

37. Bradbrook, *Malcolm Lowry: His Art and Early Life*, 29.

38. For a full reading of Lowry's 2 January 1946 letter to Jonathan

Cape, see *Selected Letters*, 57 – 88; Plomer's letter can be found in the Special Collections Library at the University of B.C.

39. Lowry, *Dark as the Grave*, 83.

40. After the Lowrys left Mexico in May 1946, Lowry chronicled their experiences in a letter to a California attorney, A. Ronald Button; see *Selected Letters*, 91 – 112.

41. See Day, 379 – 383, for a more detailed account of Lowry's trip to New York in 1947.

42. Toddy Beattie, " 'He Doesn't Like Who-Dunits But He Thinks Mine Are Good' " *The Vancouver Sun* 17 April 1947: 13; Myra Moir, review of *Under the Volcano*, by Malcolm Lowry, *Daily Province* 19 April 1947: 4.

43. Lowry's short stories "Strange Comfort Afforded by the Profession," "Elephant and Colosseum," and "Present Estate of Pompeii" were inspired by his 1947/1948 European holiday.

44. Day, *Malcolm Lowry*, 401 – 405.

NOTES TO CHAPTER THREE

1. In *The Voyage That Never Ends: Malcolm Lowry's Fiction*, Sherrill Grace examines Lowry's fiction and the relationship of the works in his planned opus. The original outline of the "Voyage," as sent to Harold Matson, is in Grace's Chapter 1.

2. Day, *Malcolm Lowry*, 419.

3. From an interview with Alfred McKee, January 1985.

4. From a telephone conversation with Mrs. Ruth Darling, former owner of the Surf Lodge, May 1985.

5. Lowry's correspondence indicates other reasons for wanting to keep their whereabouts unknown: Margerie's visa had expired and she was in the country illegally; he did not want A.B. Carey or Arthur Lowry to know that he and Margerie were living together. See *Selected Letters*, 19 – 24.

6. Downie Kirk, "More than Music: The Critic as Correspondent," *Canadian Literature* 8 (Spring, 1961): 31 – 38; also in *Malcolm Lowry: The Man And His Work*, ed. George Woodcock, 117 – 124.

7. Kirk is referring to Lowry's operation for varicose veins. Unfortunately, Kirk and Lowry never did swim the Inlet together.

8. A reference to the screenplay the Lowrys wrote, based on F. Scott Fitzgerald's *Tender Is the Night*.

9. Lowry is referring to his back brace.

10. According to a number of Lowry's Vancouver friends, Harvey Burt moved into the Lowrys' shack sometime after the Lowrys had moved to Europe.

11. Earle Birney, "Malcolm Lowry's Search for the Perfect Poem," *Poetry Canada Review* 7 (Autumn, 1985): 20. Many of Lowry's poems had alternate titles and "A Bottle From the Sea" appeared in *Atlantic Monthly* as "In Memoriam: Ingvald Bjorndal."

12. The poems published were: "Sestina in a Cantina," *Canadian Poetry Magazine* Vol. II: 1 (September, 1947): 24 – 27; "Old Freighter in an Old Port," "Port Moody," "Indian Arm," *Canadian Poetry Magazine* Vol. II: 2 (December, 1947): 24 – 25.

13. Malcolm Lowry, "Sunrise," *Outposts* 10 (Summer, 1948): 7.

14. Other Canadian editors to publish Lowry's poems were: Alan Crawley, *Contemporary Verse: A Canadian Quarterley* 21 (Summer, 1947): 3 – 5, and 24 (Spring, 1948): 6; Ralph Gustafson, *The Penguin Book of Canadian Verse* (Great Britain: Unwin Brothers Limited, 1958): 163 – 164; and A.J.M. Smith, *The Book of Canadian Poetry* (Toronto: University of Chicago Press, 1948): 371 – 375.

15. Letter written by Earle Birney (May, 1961) to New York Times reviewer Elizabeth Janeway. The letter is in the "Birney Subgroup" of the "Malcolm Lowry Collection," Special Collections (U.B.C. 52:9).

16. A reference to the work influenced by Lowry's stay in Bellevue Hospital, New York, 1936. Earle Birney and Margerie Lowry edited the novella and it was published in the *Paris Review* 29 (Winter/Spring, 1963); by Jonathan Cape (London, 1968); and in *Psalms and Songs* (New York, 1975).

17. Birney and Margerie Lowry compiled "Malcolm Lowry: A Bibliography Part I," published in *Canadian Literature* 8 (Spring, 1961): 81 – 88; "Part II" was published in 9 (Summer, 1961): 80 – 84; Birney

compiled the "Second Supplement to the Malcolm Lowry Bibliography" in 19 (Winter, 1964): 83 – 89.

18. As of 1985, *Selected Poems of Malcolm Lowry* is the only book of Lowry's poetry that has been published.

19. A copy of this documentary is on videocassette in the Special Collections Library at the University of British Columbia, (47:3).

20. In a letter written to Birney (26 March 1949), Lowry stated: "The reviews are, as well as flattering, damned interesting to me, especially the one that laid the stress on the mystical and religious catabasis traced by the Consul. This pointed out something in my intention I didn't know myself but which is certainly there. . . . All this means a lot to one" (*Selected Letters*, 177).

21. This is a reference to Lowry's ukulele. It is often referred to as a "guitar" by his Vancouver friends. For a picture of Lowry's ukulele (left with Harvey Burt) see "The Magazine," *The Vancouver Province* 23 September 1984: 3; also U.B.C. 40:6.

22. The only known tape-recording of Lowry was made by his friend Einar Neilson. He recorded Lowry singing the Canadian national anthem that Lowry had written, but the tape was accidentally erased and the words have been lost. In the 1960s Phil Thomas (see Thomas Interview) recorded Margerie singing "The Faithful Sailor-Boy" and Lowry's ballad "On A May Morning."

23. It is not clear whether Lowry's stay at the Newtons' coach house took place on a weekend or during the week: Gloria Onley recalls that it was a weekend; Norman Newton does not remember; Noel Stone says that he picked Lowry up at the Newtons', and that he and Lowry spent the weekend on Bowen Island. Also see Note 25 and Note 26.

24. It is not known what Margerie's health problems were at this time, but it is thought that she returned to Vancouver within a few days to a week of being notified of Lowry's condition.

25. Newton was working as an ambulance dispatcher and so was possibly working irregular days; he does not recall which days of the week Lowry spent at the coach house.

26. The Newtons did not have a car. Noel Stone picked Lowry up and says that Newton accompanied them to the ferry terminal. Newton has no recollection of this, but does remember looking up at Lowry who was forlornly waving goodbye as Newton rode off in a vehicle, probably a bus.

Stone and Lowry then took the ferry to Bowen Island, where they stayed with Einar and Muriel Neilson.

27. Contrary to Day, 461, Newton never lived in Dollarton and was never a student of Birney's. He was an "extramural" member of the writing group *Authors Anonymous*.

28. Lowry wrote a review of *Turvey* for the U.B.C. *Thunderbird* 5 (December 1949): 24 – 26.

29. Stone's account differs from that given by Day, 461, in which he states that the Newtons took Lowry to Bowen Island; that the Neilsons had to sit up all night with Lowry; and that they were so frightened by his behaviour that they took him to St. Paul's Hospital in Vancouver. While the Neilsons may have taken Lowry to the hospital, this did not occur until after Stone had left, and was more likely a result of noticeable pain than extreme or frightening behaviour.

30. A reference to the poem Lowry read to many of his Vancouver friends, "Sestina in a Cantina."

31. A reference to the Shell refinery and its numerous petroleum storage tanks.

32. According to Gordon Bowker's *Malcolm Lowry Remembered*, the Burts met the Lowrys in 1950; according to the following interview, reprinted from Kilgallin's book, *Lowry*, they met in 1952.

33. This is a reference to Lowry's poem "Christ walks in this infernal district too," *Selected Poems of Malcolm Lowry*, 64.

34. A book shelf used as a room divider gave the livingroom/kitchen the appearance of being two rooms.

35. Purdy's recollections up to this point are from "Lowry: A Memoir," *Books in Canada* 3 (January/February, 1974): 3 – 4.

36. Purdy's recollections up to this point are from *No Other Country* (Toronto: McClelland and Stewart, 1977), 57 – 58.

37. From Purdy's "A Memoir of Malcolm Lowry," *Canada Month* (September, 1962): 25 – 26.

38. A reference to Lowry's ukulele.

39. From a discussion with William McConnell.

40. According to Day, 425, the story was "Elephant and Colosseum," posthumously published in Lowry's collection of short stories, *Hear us O Lord from heaven thy dwelling place.*

41. In June 1951 a high school student by the name of Francis Sykes was accused of the sex slaying of a thirteen year old girl. He was found guilty and sentenced to death by hanging at Vancouver's Oakalla Prison on 11 December 1951. Hundreds of representations were sent to Ottawa requesting that the sentence be commuted. On 24 October 1951 the sentence was changed to life imprisonment.

42. The Lowrys had been on a trip through the Lake district in June 1957 but Mrs. Mason told McConnell that the Lowrys were planning a second trip.

43. Notes for McConnell's 1957 C.B.C. radio program are to be found in the "McConnell Subgroup" of the "Malcolm Lowry Collection," Special Collections (U.B.C. 1:10).

NOTES TO THE CONCLUSION

1. Interview with George Meckling, January 1985.

2. See Lowry's 22 May 1954 letter to Albert Erskine, his editor at Reynal and Hitchcock (*Selected Letters*, 370 – 372); also see Lowry's 29 April 1957 letter to the Canadian writer Ralph Gustafson (*Selected Letters*, 407 – 410).

3. Day, *Malcolm Lowry*, 11.

4. Day, *Malcolm Lowry*, 17.

5. Apomorphine aversion therapy induces sickness which the patient supposedly learns to associate with other things (e.g. alcohol), thereby inducing an "aversion." For further information on Lowry's psychological health and treatments at Atkinson Morley's, see Day's *Malcolm Lowry*, 24 – 30, 36 – 38.

6. See Lowry's July 1955 letter to Albert Erskine in *Selected Letters*, 381.

7. Lowry, *October Ferry to Gabriola*, 197.

8. Lowry, *October Ferry to Gabriola*, 65.

9. Lowry, "The Forest Path to the Spring," *Hear us O Lord*, 218, 217, 254, 216.

Selected Bibliography

PART I: WORKS BY MALCOLM LOWRY

"Bulls of the Resurrection." *Prism International* 5, 1 (Summer, 1965): 5 – 11.

China and Kristbjorg's Story: In the Black Hills. New York: Aloe Editions, 1974. Also in *Psalms and Songs*: "China," 49 – 54; "Kristbjorg's Story: In the Black Hills," 250 – 254.

"Economic Conference, 1934." *Arena* 2 (Autumn, 1949): 49 – 57.

Dark as the Grave Wherein my Friend is Laid. New York: American Library, 1968; London: Jonathan Cape, 1969; London: Penguin, 1972.

"Essays and Reviews," Review of *Turvey*, by Earle Birney. *Thunderbird* 5 (December, 1949): 24 – 26.

"Garden of Etla." *United Nations World* 4 (June, 1950): 45 – 47.

"Ghostkeeper." *American Review* 17 (Spring, 1973): 1 – 34. Also in *Psalms and Songs*, 202 – 227.

"Goya the Obscure." *The Venture* 6 (1930): 270 – 278.

Hear us O Lord from heaven thy dwelling place. Philadelphia: Lippincott, 1961; London: Jonathan Cape, 1962; London: Penguin, 1969.

"Hotel Room in Chartres." *Story* 5 (September, 1934): 53 – 58. Also in *Psalms and Songs*, 36 – 48.

"In Le Havre." *Life and Letters* 10 (July, 1934): 642 – 666.

"June the 30th, 1934." *Psalms and Songs*, 36 – 48.

Lunar Caustic. Edited by Earle Birney and Margerie Bonner Lowry. *Paris Review* 29 (Winter/Spring, 1963): 15 – 72; London: Jonathan Cape, 1968. Also in *Psalms and Songs*, 259-306.

Notes on a Screenplay for F. Scott Fitzgerald's "Tender Is the Night." Bloomfield Hills, Michigan; Columbia, South Carolina: Bruccoli Clark, 1976. The "Notes" and the screenplay were written by both Malcolm and Margerie Lowry.

October Ferry to Gabriola. New York: World Publishing, 1970; London: Penguin, 1979.

"On Board the West Hardaway." *Story* 3 (October, 1933): 12 – 22. Also in *Psalms and Songs*, 25 – 35.

"Port Swettenham." *Experiment* 5 (February, 1930): 2 – 26.

"Preface to a Novel." *Canadian Literature* 9 (Summer, 1961): 23 – 29.

Psalms and Songs. Edited by Margerie Lowry. New York and Scarborough, Ont.: New American Library, 1975.

"Punctum Indifferens Skibet Gaar Videre." *Experiment* 7 (Spring, 1931): 62 – 75. Also published under the title "Seducto ad Adsurdum," in *Best British Short Stories of 1931*, edited by E.J. O'Brien. New York: Dodd, Mead & Company, 1931, 80 – 107.

Selected Letters Of Malcolm Lowry. Edited by Harvey Breit and Margerie Bonner Lowry. Philadelphia & New York: J. B. Lippincott, 1965.

Selected Poems of Malcolm Lowry. Edited by Earle Birney. San Francisco: City Lights Books, 1962.

"The Bravest Boat." *Partisan Review* 3 (May-June, 1954): 275 – 288. Also in *Hear us O Lord from heaven thy dwelling place*, 13 – 27.

Ultramarine. London: Jonathan Cape, 1933. Revised edition. Philadelphia: Lippincott, 1962; London: Penguin, 1974.

"Under the Volcano." *Prairie Schooner* 37, (Winter, 1963 – 64): 284 – 300. Also in *Psalms and Songs.*

Under the Volcano. New York: Reynal and Hitchcock, 1947; London: Jonathan Cape, 1947; New York: Vintage-Random House, 1958; London: Penguin, 1962; Philadelphia: J. B. Lippincott, 1965; New York: Signet, 1965.

The Special Collections Library of the University of British Columbia holds most of Lowry's original manuscripts and notebooks; correspondence "incoming" and "outgoing" for Malcolm and Margerie Lowry; personal papers including copies of his certificate of marriage to Margerie Bonner, and his death certificate; a large collection of photographs; many books from Lowry's personal library; memorabilia; and a collection of "Subgroups" related to Lowry.

Aiken, Conrad. "Malcolm Lowry: A Note." *Canadian Literature* 8 (Spring, 1961): 29 – 30; also in *Malcolm Lowry: The Man And His Work*, edited by George Woodcock, 101 – 102.

————. *Ushant: An Essay.* London: W. H. Allen, 1963.

Birney, Earle and Lowry, Margerie. "Malcolm Lowry: A Bibliography: Part I." *Canadian Literature* 8 (Spring, 1961): 81 – 88, and "Part II" 9 (Summer, 1961): 80 – 84.

Birney, Earle. Guest editor, *Outposts* 10 (Summer, 1948): 7.

————. "Second Supplement to the Malcolm Lowry Bibliography." *Canadian Literature* 19 (Winter, 1964): 83 – 89.

————. "The Unknown Poetry Of Malcolm Lowry." *British Columbia Library Quarterly* 24, 4 (April, 1961): 33 – 40; also in *Malcolm Lowry: the writer & his critics*, edited by Barry Wood. Ottawa, Canada: The Tecumseh Press, 1980, 194 – 199.

————. *Spreading Time: Remarks on Canadian Writing and Writers: 1904 – 1949.* Montreal: Vehicule Press, 1980.

————. "Malcolm Lowry's Search for the Perfect Poem." *Poetry Canada Review* 7 (Autumn, 1985): 3 – 4, 20 – 21.

Bonner, Margerie. *The Shapes that Creep.* New York: Scribner, 1946.

————. *The Last Twist of the Knife.* New York: Charles Scribner's Sons, 1946.

————. *Horse in the Sky.* New York: Charles Scribner's Sons, 1947.

Bowker, Gordon. *Malcolm Lowry Remembered.* London: Ariel Books, 1985.

Bradbrook, M. C. *Malcolm Lowry: His Art and Early Life.* Cambridge: Cambridge University Press, 1974.

Crawley, Alan, ed. *Contemporary Verse: A Canadian Quarterly.* 21 (Summer, 1947), and 24 (Spring, 1948).

Day, Douglas. *Malcolm Lowry: A Biography.* New York: Oxford University Press, 1973.

Dollar, Robert. *Memoirs of Robert Dollar* Volume II. San Francisco: W.S. Van Cott & Co., 1921.

Epstein, Pearl. *The Private Labyrinth of Malcolm Lowry: Under the Volcano and the Cabbala.* New York: Holt, Rinehart & Winston, 1969.

Graham, Donald. *Keepers of the Light: A History of British Columbia's Lighthouses and Their Keepers.* Madeira Park, B.C.: Harbour Publishing Co. Ltd., 1985.

Grace, Sherrill. *The Voyage That Never Ends: Malcolm Lowry's Fiction.* Vancouver: University of British Columbia Press, 1982.

————. "Margerie Bonner's Three Forgotten Novels." *Journal of Modern Literature* 6 (April 1977): 321 – 324.

Gustafson, Ralph, ed. *The Penguin Book of Canadian Verse.* Woking and London: Unwin Brothers Limited, 1958.

Haldane, Charlotte. *I Bring Not Peace.* London: Chatto & Windus, 1931.

Kilgallin, Tony. *Lowry.* Erin, Ont.: Press Porcépic, 1973.

Kirk, Downie. "More Than Music: The Critic as Correspondent." *Canadian Literature* 8 (Spring, 1961): 31 – 38; also in *Malcolm Lowry: The Man And His Work*, edited by George Woodcock, 117 – 124.

Lowry, Margerie. Review of *Notes From the Century Before: A Journal From British Columbia, by Edward Hoaglund.* New York: Ballantine Books, 1972, ©1969.

Lowry, Russell. "Preface: Malcolm—A Closer Look." In *The Art Of Malcolm Lowry*, edited by Anne Smith. London: Vision Press, 1978, p. 9 – 27.

McConnell, William. "In Search Of The Word." *The Malcolm Lowry Review* 17 & 18 (Fall 1985 & Spring 1986): 25 – 36.

————. "Recollections of Malcolm Lowry." *Canadian Literature* 6 (Autumn, 1960): 24 – 30; also in *Masks of Fiction: Canadian Writers on Canadian Prose*, edited by A.J.M. Smith and Malcolm Ross. Toronto: McClelland and Stewart Limited, 1961, pp. 141 – 150; and *Malcolm Lowry: The Man And His Work*, edited by George Woodcock, 154 – 162.

McNeill, C. G. "Malcolm Lowry Visits the Doctor." *American Review* 17 (Spring, 1973): 35 – 39; also in *Psalms and Songs*, edited by Margerie Lowry, 102 – 105.

Mercer, Michael. *Goodnight Disgrace*. Dir. Leon Pownall. With Graeme Campbell and Ron Hadler. The Vancouver Playhouse, Vancouver, B.C., September 1985.

—————. *Goodnight Disgrace. Canadian Theatre Review* 41 (Winter 1984): 73 – 131.

—————. Lecture given in "A Canadian Play in Context Series," sponsored by the University of British Columbia, 1985.

New, William. *Malcolm Lowry: A Reference Guide*. Boston: G.K. Hall, 1978.

Noram Group of Consultants. *The First Fifty Years: Shellburn 1932-1982*. Vancouver: Shell Canada Limited, 1982.

Noxon, Gerald. "In Connection With Malcolm Lowry." Transcript of 1961 American radio broadcast, published by Paul G. Tiessen in *The Malcolm Lowry Review* 17 & 18 (Fall 1985 & Spring 1986): 10 – 24.

Purdy, Al. *No Other Country*. Toronto: McClelland and Stewart, 1977.

—————. "Malcolm Lowry," *The Cariboo Horses*. Toronto: McClelland and Stewart, 1965, 9 – 10.

—————. "About Pablum, Teachers, And Malcolm Lowry," *The Crafte So Longe to Learne*. Toronto: Ryerson Press, 1959, 7 – 8.

—————. "Lowry: A Memoir." *Books in Canada* 3 (January/February, 1974): 3 – 4.

—————. "A Memoir of Malcolm Lowry." *Canada Month* (September, 1962): 25 – 26.

Robertson, George. *Malcolm Lowry: To the Volcano (Part 1); The Forest Path (Part 2)*. Canadian Broadcasting Corporation, 1961.

Salloum, Sheryl. "Eridanus: Another View." *The Malcolm Lowry Review* 17 & 18 (Fall 1985 & Spring 1986): 37 – 53.

Smith, A.J.M., ed. *The Book of Canadian Poetry*. Toronto: University of Chicago Press, 1948.

Smith, Anne, ed. *The Art Of Malcolm Lowry*. London: Vision Press, 1978.

Taylor, G. W. *Timber: History of the Forest Industry in B.C.* Vancouver: J.J. Douglas Ltd., 1975.

Thomas, Hilda. "Malcolm Lowry's *Under the Volcano*: an interpretation." Master's thesis, University of British Columbia, 1965.

———. "Lowry's Letters." Review article in *Canadian Literature* 29 (Summer, 1966): 56 – 58.

———. "Lowry's Letters." In *Malcolm Lowry: The Man And His Work*, edited by George Woodcock, 103 – 109.

Tiessen, Paul G. "Introduction" to Malcolm Lowry's *Notes on a Screenplay for F. Scott Fitzgerald's "Tender Is the Night."*

———. "The Daily Province, 1939: Lowry and Film." In *The Malcolm Lowry Newsletter* 10 (Spring, 1982): 11 – 13.

———. "Editor's Note 4." *Malcolm Lowry Newsletter* 11 (Fall, 1982): 3.

———, ed. *The Malcolm Lowry Review* (formerly *The Malcolm Lowry Newsletter*), published biannually by the Department of English, Wilfrid Laurier University, Waterloo, Ontario, Canada.

Wood, Barry, ed. *Malcolm Lowry: the man & his critics*. Ottawa, Canada: The Tecumseh Press, 1980.

Woodcock, George, ed. *Malcolm Lowry: The Man And His Work*. Vancouver: University of British Columbia Press, 1971.

Woodward-Reynolds, Kathleen Marjorie. "A History of the City and District of North Vancouver." Master's thesis, University of British Columbia, 1943.

Woolmer, Howard J. *Malcolm Lowry: A Bibliography*. Revere, Pennsylvania: Woolmer Brotherson Ltd., 1983.

Index